MW01087201

BARACK OBAMA

&

LARRY SINCLAIR

Cocaine, Sex, Lies & Murder?

By Lawrence W. Sinclair

First Published by Sinclair Publishing, Inc. 2009

Cataloging-in-Publication data on file with the Library of Congress

ISBN: 978-0-615-34506-2

Library of Congress Control Number: 2009902125

Published in the United States by

Sinclair Publishing, Inc
9 Spring Dr
Port Orange, Florida 32129
386-761-0606

Manufactured in the United States of America

10 9 8 7 6 5 4 3 2

In Memory of
Donald Young

This book,

BARACK OBAMA & LARRY SINCLAIR
Cocaine, Sex, Lies & Murder?

is dedicated to the memory of Donald Young, a man who died for no other reason than to protect the image of Barack Obama. His early demise prevented the world from knowing the truth about Barack Obama, which is that he is a closet homosexual, the likes of Jim McGreevy and Ted Haggard.

A very special *Thank You* to all those Americans, who simply asked for the media to report the truth about Barack Obama, and who quickly realized that would not happen in this new era of media bias. For the Black, White, Asian, Latino, Italian, Irish, etc., people who have refused to be threatened, bullied and intimidated by the Obama thugs.

CONTENTS

Foreword
By Jeff Rense

When Larry Sinclair invited me to write the foreword to this book, I immediately accepted. Yes, his is an unusually strange and volatile story but Mr. Sinclair has every right under the U.S. Constitution to present his allegations against President Obama to the public and the world. Without Freedom of Speech, our nation is finished.

Having spent 15 years interviewing and listening to thousands of some of the most unusual and remarkable people on the planet, I have heard many truly incredible stories. Nothing much surprises me anymore. I listen...extremely carefully...to each and every person on my program and, although I've been deceived on rare occasions, I have a very good sense of someone's moral truth, credibility...and devotion to reality as they know it. Larry Sinclair demonstrates all of these qualities and more.

I first presented Larry as a guest on the program January 23, 2008, just a few weeks after Donald Young was murdered in his Chicago apartment on December 23, 2007. Donald was the gay choirmaster at Barack Obama's Chicago church and had initiated what turned into frequent email and phone contact with Larry about his allegations and inquiring about what he planned to do

1

with them. Donald reportedly told Larry, in no uncertain terms, he was calling on behalf of Obama and that Obama had provided Larry's private cell phone number to him. In all probability, Donald Young was murdered to silence him. This astonishing story is but one of many in Mr. Sinclair's book which underscore how much power... and darkness...are behind the Obama Presidency.

Since that first radio program and all through the (contrived) Presidential Campaign of 2008, I followed the Sinclair-Obama story carefully and closely. In fact, to date, I have had Larry on the program as a guest more than 20 times in order to track the story as carefully and completely as possible. No one - not one person from the Obama campaign - has accepted my standing invitation to appear on my program to refute any of the Sinclair allegations.

In over two decades of broadcast journalism, Larry Sinclair's humility, courage and steadfast adherence to his allegations have few equals in my professional experience. Not once has Larry backed away from his contentions of what he claims transpired between him and Obama, twice in 1999, in any way, shape or form.

Without question, if America was being served by a true, honest and legitimate main stream press, the biggest story of the 2008 (manipulated) presidential 'campaign' season would have been the story of Larry Sinclair and his charges that Obama engaged in homosexual sex and felony cocaine purchasing and distribution. Certainly, Obama's outrageous birth and citizenship issues would be right up there, but I submit cocaine dealing and use, and gay sex, would eclipse all else. Unfortunately, the nation's press is anything but the free and dedicated servant of the public it is supposed to be.

What happened to Larry Sinclair reads like a major Hollywood screenplay. It is said that truth is stranger than fiction...and the Sinclair story fits that expression perfectly. This remarkable book, told in Larry's own style, will take the reader through his childhood, his realization early on that he is gay, and the many mistakes and poor life choices he has made along the way. Nothing is withheld, nothing is hidden. In fact, the world knows far, far more about Larry Sinclair's life and health than it will likely ever know about the President of the most powerful nation on the planet.

Larry's story will lay it all on the line...and it is a stunning story. Is it true? That, ultimately, is your decision and your right to determine. From my perspective, I have found the story and the man telling it to be more than compelling and would not have written this introduction if I did not hold him in high regard.

Shakespeare once wrote about 'protesting too much'...and that expression certainly fits the efforts by the Obama camp and many of his fanatical disciples who have spared no effort to shut Larry Sinclair up.

Rather than laugh him off and ignore him, the Obama machine and its hardcore operatives, volunteers and just plain kooks have been so afraid of him that their behavior and efforts to smear him alone lend even more credibility to Larry's allegations.

In fact, the attacks on Sinclair over the internet, by phone and through other channels add up to a nearly incessant stream of some of the most vile, public, nationwide and worldwide personal attacks I've ever seen thrown at anyone. The number of character assaults and death threats...some even on YouTube...suggest quite clearly that someone is trying very hard to bury Larry Sinclair's Constitutional rights to air his allegations.

As most who have followed the story know, Larry Sinclair's original efforts to get Obama to step forward were confined to his purported use of crack cocaine in 1999, far more recently than the official Obama drug use statements claim.

As you may also know, Sinclair's raising the issue of homo-sexual relations with Obama in his allegations came about later and stemmed from the murdered Donald Young's phone and email conversations with Sinclair; contacts allegedly initiated by Obama himself.

Perhaps we shouldn't call it the 'Obama Machine' because it is far more than that. Barky is, of course, just a sock puppet of the Globalist New World Order...the perfect 'Rock Star' Celebrity President for a society hopelessly devolved into a People Maga-zine, MTV, Pop Culture waste dump of programmed immorality and trash.

As soon as Larry Sinclair began to make 'noise' on the net and on my program, the Obama power base immediately organ-ized a clearly high-level, multi-faceted assault on him featuring bizarre events like top advisor David Axelrod allegedly hiring internet porn merchant, Don Parisi, of the otherwise commercial porn site, Whitehouse.com, to set up an embarrassingly rigged polygraph 'examination' of Larry which he graciously made him-self available for. The test, as you will read, was administered by the strange and rather shady Edward I. Gelb, polygraph examiner for hire, who among other things represented himself as having a Ph.D. when he apparently does not.

In this most revealing story of Larry Sinclair standing his ground against an array of attackers, Obots, government agents and compromised and corrupted public officials, you'll also read of the disgusting, multiple, ongoing character attacks and criminal death threats, he and his family have had to endure...and the truly outrageous dereliction of duty by law enforcement, both Federal and local, in dealing with these interstate felony assaults.

Then there is the possible conspiracy of now Vice President Joe "I am a Zionist!" Biden and his son, Delaware Attorney General Beau Biden, who issued a contrived warrant resulting in the arrest and incarceration of Larry literally moments after completing his National Press Club news conference in Washington, D.C.

Furthermore, let's not omit the refusal of the Chicago Police Department to investigate Rev. Jeremiah Wright and Barack Obama and their possible involvement in the murder of Donald Young.

The litany of nightmares Larry Sinclair has stood up to would have shredded the average individual. Some of the Obama cabal have tried to impugn him by saying he has profited greatly from his claims and allegations. Having covered the entire matter from the beginning, I have seen nothing whatever to indicate Larry has profited from his allegations, beyond some modest public donations to help him maintain his internet site and travel to support his efforts to bring his story to the public. This book is his first 'revenue-producing' effort to date. A true hustler would have been hawking DVDs and books long ago.

So, again, as you read this astonishing book, prepare to think about it honestly and logically...for it will challenge you to do just that. The Larry Sinclair story is utterly unique on the American Political Landscape. Is it true? Again, that is for you to decide. One thing I guarantee...you will never forget it.

Introduction

In the year when the first person of color (a mulatto) was elected to become President of the United States, the biggest story of all was carefully and completely suppressed by the Mainstream Media, the power brokers who control the man involved, and the American political process. This story is stunning to most, so much so that many simply refuse to believe it despite all of the proof and evidence that the events you will read about, indeed, occurred.

Aside from a few courageous talk radio programs, some internet sites which practice genuine journalism, some of the American tabloid press; Barack Hussein Obama received a free ticket to ride. He was never the subject of one single major media investigation regarding what you are about to read in this account. This story is about what could have, and what should have, been front page banner headlines in every major print and electronic outlet in America.

Yes, the story is sensational, but it is absolutely true. You will read in detail, specific detail, about how Barack Hussein Obama engaged in homosexual encounters and used crack co-caine while serving in the Illinois State Senate in 1999. The story further details the "Obama Machine's" efforts to keep these events completely out of the national media; efforts that included death threats, false arrest warrants, misuse of the legal system, massive smear and character defamation operations and many other down and dirty sordid attempts to subvert the truth.

It simply would never have occurred to me in a million years that a couple of nights of casual sex and coke use with a man in Chicago on November 6 and 7, 1999, would have turned into the biggest unreported story of the 2008 U.S. Presidential campaign and election.

This book represents my utter commitment to the truth and to tell the story of my experiences with Barack Obama, what subsequently happened to me and my family and just about anyone else who demanded and sought accountability from Obama and his campaign. This book tells the full story of my experiences. It will make clear the distorted and misrepresented trash the hardcore Obot agents and internet junkyards like, Politico.com, Dailykos.com, HuffingtonPost.com and DemocraticUnderground.com, have relentlessly promoted during the election.

I am not, nor have I ever been, what one would consider a model citizen. I have been forthright about that. Yes, I have my past indiscretions, yes, I have made mistakes in life, but I have always admitted to them and accepted responsibility for my actions. In fact, I fully disclosed my past behaviors from the very beginning of this entire, now infamous, Sinclair versus Obama story.

My life, for a number of reasons, was rather colorful from childhood on into early adulthood. You will read about those years and experiences in the pages ahead. In this book, you will also discover the hidden truth, again in very specific detail, about a secret, hidden portion of the life led by Barack Hussein Obama. I will also tell about the lengths, he and those around him have gone to, in order to keep the truth hidden. However, unlike Barack Obama, I do not live my life…and then try and hide from it later.

Chapter One
Who Is Larry Sincl

I was born Tuesday, September 26, 1 third of four children to Hubert and Mary Sir South Carolina. I sometimes believe I was bo

At a very young age, it was apparent th a force to be reckoned with in the south. At a tion and racial hatred were the norm, I became "queer" of the county. As a child I was determ gardless of what that meant to anyone else. W for boys were GI Joes, trucks and cars, I threw tantrums until my wishes for tea sets and Easy l met. However, my temper was not confined to As a child, my temper raised many an eyebrow i Baptist region. My mother had Baptist ministers seek out a Catholic priest to perform exorcisms o family or friend, ever understood where a kid so ; gained the foul vocabulary that I had mastered by

Along with my temper also came an above av gence. I knew I was gay by the age of seven, and ter a psychiatrist (the only one in my life, I have ev

ct for) with the Medical College Hospital in Charleston,
h Carolina, advised both my mother and father that I was
Unlike today, most parents would freak out and try to come
ith ways to convert their kid if they discovered they had a
son. You would expect that in the 1960's, but that never hap-
d with me and my parents. During my entire childhood, my
g gay was one of the (least talked about) clearly known se-
s in the Camden community.

Even though I was openly gay at a young age, I was not the
sy" gay that most people think of. I enjoyed boxing, as well
aseball, football and other physical activities. I was a hyper-
ve child who decided at a young age to be the captain of my
n ship.

After several explosions of my temper in the public school
ting it became clear that I was going to be a difficult child.
hen I lost my temper it was as if something, or someone, had
tered my body and taken over. My physical strength would
crease to that of many grown men. During one incident while
ing in Hartsville, South Carolina, several adults had to physi-
lly pry my hands off of my younger sister's neck. It was just
ter this that my mother and the pastor from Calvary Baptist
hurch took me to Columbia, South Carolina and admitted me to
e South Carolina State Hospital.

14

I was put on Ritalin, but it made me more hyperactive, so that was changed to the medication Mellaril. In this time period, doctors loved to label kids "emotionally disturbed." To this day no one has ever been able to explain just what "emotionally disturbed" means. After a brief stay in Columbia, it was decided that a program at the Medical College Hospital in Charleston, South Carolina was better suited to "help" me.

My childhood continued from one school to another; from John De La Howe School in McCormick, South Carolina, to the South Carolina School for Boys in Florence, South Carolina, to Sacred Heart in Pueblo, Colorado, to VisionQuest in Tucson, Arizona (where I eventually got my high school diploma and started my first enrollment in college at Cochise College in Douglas, Arizona), until I simply decided to take control in early adulthood.

From childhood into my teenage years, I was always some place other than home. I often joked with family about how I managed to go through my entire childhood without ever appearing in a single yearbook or having one school picture taken of me.

At the age of 18, I decided it was time for me to strike out, away from everyone and everything to find my own way. After getting a job at Pizza Hut in Denver, Colorado on South Broadway, I soon realized how easy it was for me to be obsessed with

doing a good job. After a short period of time, I had started clos-
ing, doing the books weekly, and before I knew it I was promoted
to assistant manager. Until one day, when I had enough and just
walked out. It was still a good learning experience. Up to this
point in my life, I had never gotten into the "gay" scene. I had
always been openly gay but never felt the need to bar hop and
hang with a group. I should have kept feeling that way.

In early 1980 I gave in to living the gay scene. I began going out to the clubs, hanging with all the drama queens and the
late night/early morning restaurant visits after the clubs closed. I
began writing checks that lacked funds to cover them, from White
-Spot to the Old Grist Mill. I even started getting into the gay
clothing scene, where I was writing NSF checks to stores in the
Denver area such as MAX, to purchase the latest styles in the gay
scene. This living in the gay culture in Denver in 1980 would be
the beginning of my early adult mistakes that would result in
criminal charges and convictions. To this day, the Obama Machine has used and misrepresented my past in efforts to make me
look less than honest in my revelations about him.

While I have always been open and honest about my life and
actions, I feel it necessary to explain my past in the order that it
took place, and as it took place, rather than how the Obama surrogates represented it during the entire year of 2008. You will find

in the next chapter, the extent of my past and will also learn that contrary to the claims by the Obama surrogates, I have only lived under and been known by three (3) names (all of which were legal), and not the fourteen the Obama people had Politico.com and other media outlets falsely report.

Chapter Two
Early Adulthood Mistakes

It was in the late spring/early summer of 1980, while grow-ing tired of the constant drama associated with the gay scene in Denver, I borrowed a friend's car and drove to Arizona. After arriving in Tucson, I went to visit with a former counselor from my days in VisionQuest (a youth program started by Bob Burton and his wife, that's based on the Plains Indian's transformation from childhood to adulthood). It was during this visit that I took a book of checks belonging to a VisionQuest counselor, and started cashing them at the local 7-Eleven. Within a week, I left Tucson and drove to Bisbee/Douglas, Arizona to visit with a former counselor and lover named Oscar De La Rosa.

When I arrived in Douglas, I found out from Oscar's mom that he was in the Cochise County Jail in Bisbee. I contacted the jail and set up an attorney visit with him. I had, for whatever the reason, decided to tell the jail that I was Oscar's attorney. After visiting Oscar in jail, I returned to Douglas where I had gotten a room at the Gadsden Hotel. All the while, I was paying for the room and everything else with checks from the VisionQuest counselor's checkbook. A few days later, I was arrested and charged with forgery and theft in Cochise County Arizona, under my true name Lawrence Wayne Sinclair.

The court appointed Ruben Teran as my attorney, and as I had always done my entire life when caught, I pled guilty to the charges against me and was sentenced to four years in the Arizona Department of Corrections.

Shortly after arriving at the Arizona Department of Correction's Reception and Classification Center (aka Alhambra) in Phoenix, I was informed that there was a detainer warrant from Denver County, Colorado for a theft charge. I filed the required paperwork for Denver to pick up and dispose of the charges within the 180 days set by law. I completed my classification and was initially assigned to the Central Unit of the Arizona Department of Corrections in Florence, Arizona.

Upon my arrival at the Central Unit, I met a guy named Tomas Silvas, who I immediately fell in love with and began a relationship with. Tomas was a member of the MM, also known as the Mexican Mafia. It was shortly after this relationship began that the Aryan Brotherhood (AB), Mau Mau and the MM began planning a race battle for who was entitled to the new queen on the block; the new queen being me. I was completely unaware of the racial cliques at the ADOC.

When the AB, the "White Supremists", the Mau Mau (the Black Power), the MM and La Familia (Mexican Nationals) wanted to avoid an all out war, someone would "drop a kite" without signing it, and give it to the warden warning him/her that a fight was brewing over a "queen." They did this because they knew that the prison authorities would immediately place the "queen" in administrative protective custody against their will, avoiding a full out race war. Well, that's exactly what happened with me. Tomas and I had just spent the day together in his cell when the Correctional Officer for Cell Block 3 came to my cell and took me to the Yard Office. The Major then advised me that I was being placed in administrative protective custody.

After being removed from the "general population", I was picked up by Denver County, Colorado authorities per their request for speedy trial. This was for the disposition of the charges resulting from my writing NSF checks to the clothing store "Max." I pled guilty to the charges, as I always did when I was guilty, and was sentenced to four years of unsupervised probation to run concurrently with my Arizona sentence.

Following my return from Colorado, I decided to show Tomas I was committed to my relationship with him. The "cliques" in the prison were determined to keep us apart with their "shooting of kites" and threatening violence, if I was allowed to remain in general population. To prove to Tomas how much I cared for him, I legally took his last name and filed a Petition for Name Change in the Penal County Superior Court in Florence, Arizona. I changed my name from Lawrence Wayne Sinclair to La-Rye Ashaiti Silvas. This name change petition was granted by the Penal County Superior Court, the Arizona Department of Corrections and the Social Security Administration. Subsequently, they changed their records to reflect the legally obtained name change. I even tattooed "Tomas" on my left arm where it remains to this day.

I was eventually paroled in 1982 shortly before my twenty -first birthday. My first Arizona driver's license was issued under my legal name, La-Rye Ashaiti Silvas. I had written to Marriott Hotel's Camelback Inn in Scottsdale, Arizona prior to my parole seeking employment, and upon my release, I obtained employment with the Camelback Inn.

In early 1983, my parole was revoked after a former female roommate and co-worker from the Marriott Camelback Inn, falsely claimed I was in possession of a handgun. She knowingly made these claims after she became the subject of much talk and ridicule at work. She tried to "turn me straight" at a party one night, where she thought because I was drunk I would want to have sex with her. Only it did not go the way she planned. The only thing she got was me throwing up on her when she revealed her naked body.

After my return to custody, I met Frank Vizcarra Avila, with whom I became involved in a very serious and loving relationship. Again, I took the proper legal action in a Petition for Name Change filed in the Penal County Arizona Superior Court changing my legal name of La-Rye Ashaiti Silvas to La-Rye Vizcarra Avila. I kept this name throughout most of my adult life. Upon completing my Arizona sentence, I returned to Phoenix and my name change was recorded with Arizona DOC, DMV and with Social Security. My second Arizona and first Colorado Driver's License were issued under my legal name of La-Rye Vizcarra Avila.

After going to work for Tony Roma's in Scottsdale, Arizona, I moved to North Hollywood in Southern California. I went to work for the company-owned Tony Roma's in Encino and Beverly Hills, before being promoted to chef/kitchen manager at the Santa Monica location. I noticed that the Mexican employees, who had been there longer and had more experience, were being paid a great deal less than their white or black counterparts. I had a difference of opinion with the district manager about their low pay. I left California and moved to New York.

I first resided in Rego Park, Queens and then later in Forest Hills and Long Island City (also in Queens). I went to work with the Waldorf-Astoria and part-time with Tony Roma's in the Village. After less than a year, I returned to Colorado and opened the Westin Tabor Center Hotel while operating my own small catering business.

It was after leaving Colorado, going to South Florida and an adventure with a fling named Carlos, that I committed theft by taking. I used the American Express number of my former co-worker and friend Stuart Kochel by sending myself money via Western Union over the phone. I was arrested in a motel by the Miami-Dade police and taken to the Broward County, Ft. Lauderdale, Florida jail. Once again, I was guilty, so I pled guilty and was sentenced to one year and a day in the Florida Department of Corrections. I served and discharged my entire sentence at the Brevard Correctional Institution in Cocoa, Florida.

Upon my release, I went to Ft. Lauderdale and went to work for the Pier 66 Hotel and Marina. After a while, in Ft. Lauderdale, I moved to Kissimmee and then commuted to Ft. Lauderdale to work for a friend, Dan Boza, who had just purchased a diner and asked me to run his kitchen for him. I had met Dan through my Ft. Lauderdale attorney, Freeman Mark. After a few months and with the business not being what Dan had expected it to be, I decided to move to Miami Beach.

I went to Miami Beach with nothing. For the first couple of nights, I slept and showered on the beach a few blocks away from the infamous Wolfie's and Rooney's Pubs. I got a job as a waiter at Rooney's Pub on my second day in Miami and then rented a studio apartment on the 3200 block of Collins Ave. As Passover approached, I began to think about working at one of the hotels the holiday. I got on at the Shelborne Hotel on Miami Beach. Passover was a time where good servers could make in excess of twenty thousand dollars in the nine day period. Passover 1986 was a good one for me as well.

It was in the early summer of 1986 that I had been using worthless checks to pay my J.C. Penney credit card bill and then charged items up to the new credit limit. These actions resulted in my arrest by Miami-Dade Florida police and my eventual pleading guilty to forgery and theft charges, resulting in a sentence of probation for a term of one year. After completing my sentence, I returned to Miami Beach and went to live in a studio apartment at the Century Hotel. The owners and their sons Hector and Raphael were friends of mine. I went back to work for Wolfie's on Collins Avenue.

It was shortly after this that I had developed a serious case of pneumonia from my past period of smoking crack cocaine. I had already ended the use of the drug but had not realized I had been ill for some time. I took a city bus to the Emergency Room at Mt. Sinai Medical Center and had passed out in a wheelchair just as a nurse had gotten one for me. After spending a little more than two weeks in the hospital, I returned to my apartment. A friend of mine had been working for the old Ankara Motel and had been recording names, credit card numbers, driver's license information and expiration dates on guests who had stayed there. It was one of those credit card numbers that I used to purchase an airline ticket to Denver, Colorado in October, 1986.

Prior to leaving for Denver from Miami, I contacted the Lakewood Colorado Sheraton Hotel, claiming to be the owner of the credit card and arranged for the card to be used to pay for all room, food and beverage charges for La-Rye V. Avila which in 1986 was my legal name. The Sheraton accepted the authorization for the reservation and billing instructions. Upon my arrival at Denver's Stapleton International Airport, I was picked up by the hotel and checked into my room.

While staying at the Lakewood Sheraton, I never signed any name on any room charge authorization except mine. I was approached by Lakewood Colorado police officers after about a week at the hotel, and I admitted immediately that I had called the hotel claiming to be the owner of the credit card. I was arrested and charged in Jefferson County Colorado District Court where I informed Judge Shannon that I was guilty, and that he might consider sentencing me to the maximum allowed by law, because I would continue to do what I chose to do until I decided to change. After entering my formal guilty plea, I questioned Judge Shannon as to why I was being accused of forgery since the only name I ever signed was my own. That matter was dismissed by the Court of Appeals since it was not challenged in the allowed time frame.

I was sentenced to sixteen years in the Colorado Department of Corrections on each count to run concurrently. I was transferred to the Department of Corrections in April, 1987 where I remained until November, 1997.

In 1996, I was informed that my father, Lawrence Hubert Sinclair had relapsed with melanoma (cancer) and was not expected to live long. I had, upon hearing the news, filed a Petition for Name Change with the Fremont County Colorado Court to change my name from La-Rye Vizcarra Avila back to my given birth name of Lawrence Wayne Sinclair. That petition was granted in early 1997, several months after my father passed away.

Since my release in November of 1997 on parole from the Colorado Department of Corrections, I have used a single name, my legal name Lawrence (Larry) Wayne Sinclair, that of my birth. My life on parole started slow. I went to work and to school full time from 1997 until I met my friend and new room-mate Ramon Caraveo in the fall of 1998. It was after Ramon and I met and became roommates that my involvement in the selling of large amounts of drugs began. That's what made it possible for, "How Larry Met Barry!"

Chapter Three
How Larry Met Barry

The year began with me entering my second year on parole from my 1986 guilty plea for using another person's credit card number without authorization from Jefferson County, Colorado.

In early 1999, I was asked to help my best friend and roommate Ramon Caraveo's mother out. Ramon's mother trafficked in marijuana and cocaine from New Mexico to Colorado and North Carolina. Because of the policy of law enforcement in Arkansas and Tennessee of stopping and searching vehicles with New Mexico, Arizona and Texas plates driven by Hispanics, Ramon's mom, using the name Mary Lu Dominguez (a name provided to her by a friend employed by New Mexico DMV who provided drivers licenses to illegal's), asked Ramon to see if I would be willing to make a delivery for her to her nephew in Greensboro, North Carolina.

It was with this request that I got involved with moving large quantities of drugs across the country. Before this time, I had not trafficked nor sold drugs.

In my entire life, I had never been a drug user except for a couple of times experimenting with smoking a joint that made me goofy and silly, a single hit of acid in 1980 that made me cry all night, a period of smoking rock over a month's time in 1986 and doing a few lines of coke. I have never been addicted to any drug or alcohol at any point in my life.

I agreed to make this delivery for Mary Lu. It was during this delivery that I became aware of the amount of money she was making and realized I was taking all the risks. I delivered two kilos of cocaine and collected forty-eight thousand dollars in payment for Mary Lu. Over the course of a few months, I had become an asset to her. I was collecting on deliveries that she could not collect on; delivering vehicles that had all four tires packed with welded triangles inside the rims all the way around with marijuana. The gas tank and bumpers were also packed with three and four kilos of cocaine.

Mary Lu then had problems with her business in Colorado when one of her biggest distributors were raided and refused to pay her the money they owed. It turned out that Mary Lu was wanted in Arizona by law enforcement and was also in trouble with her suppliers for shorting them money. At the same time, her nephew in Greensboro, North Carolina was being watched by the law and had become a heavy user of her product.

Mary Lu had to move out of Albuquerque after crossing her suppliers. Her nephew in Greensboro was too hot to conduct business, so they had agreed that he would introduce her to his customers, and she would move to North Carolina to sell cocaine in quantity.

In June of 1999, Mary Lu moved to Greensboro and rented a house with her boyfriend Raul and her niece. After her arrival, her nephew was at a local hotel with the guys that had moved her furniture from New Mexico to North Carolina. Local law enforcement had been watching the nephew and movers for a couple of days before pulling them over. Mary Lu's niece was at the rental home and had been partying the night before with these same guys. The niece had already been arrested and convicted in Oklahoma for smuggling over a hundred pounds of marijuana and in fact, was not supposed to even be in the United States. During that party, they were doing lines of cocaine and had left a plate of cocaine on top of the fridge.

While there were no drugs in the trucks with the nephew and movers when law enforcement pulled them over while en route to

Mary Lu's rental home, the nephew knew he was going to be arrested if he did not do something, so in an effort to buy him more time, he offered to tell law enforcement where they could find drugs. The nephew then took Greensboro Police to Mary Lu's house.

The niece was at the home and police asked if they could come in (at this time they had no search warrant). With permission of the niece, the Greensboro Police entered the home and upon seeing the plate of cocaine atop the fridge, they immediately stopped and sealed the area and obtained a search warrant. After securing the search warrant, more than one kilo of cocaine was found in the home and the nephew, niece and movers were arrested.

Mary Lu and Raul were tipped off that the police were at the home and immediately left North Carolina for Kansas City. I received a call from Mary Lu asking me to immediately go to North Carolina and recover her papers, ID and get her niece out of jail before she started talking. I went to South Carolina with my childhood friend David, and then headed to Greensboro, North Carolina where I recovered most of Mary Lu's belongings and secured the release of her niece. I also secured legal counsel for Mary Lu and Raul.

It was during this trip that I happened to have about a half pound of marijuana with me. David took some of it to a friend of his who loved it. At this time, pot heads in South Carolina were paying up to a hundred sixty dollars an ounce, and that's a lot. In Colorado, it was selling for about four hundred a pound. Thus another new job was born.

After returning to Colorado, I began arranging for one to two trips per month to South Carolina with marijuana orders ranging from a low of one hundred pounds, to a high of eight hundred pounds, and cocaine orders from a low of a quarter kilo, or nine ounces, to a high of three kilos. It was in July, August, September and October that I began doing business on a regular basis with my childhood friends from South Carolina, David and Curt.

While in Camden, South Carolina, making a delivery to my friend David Dukes, Lee (David's nephew and my self-proclaimed God son) told me he was joining the Navy. Lee is the son of David's brother Ricky.

A few weeks before Ricky graduated from high school, he was killed in a car accident by Lake Wateree. Lee was born after Ricky's untimely death and raised by Ricky and David's parents, David and Delma Dukes. I first met Lee when he was about four years old, and he was the mirror image of his father.

As Lee became older and I started visiting Camden more often, we became close. I had been unable to be at Lee's high school graduation the previous May. When Lee told me he would soon be leaving for Navy Basic Training, he asked if I would be at his graduation. I swore to Lee, I would be there no matter what. Lee had already forgiven me for missing his high school graduation. I made a promise that I would not let anything keep me from his graduation from basic training, and I kept that promise.

Between September and the first of November, 1999, I kept in touch with Lee while making deliveries to his Uncle David. It was while on one of my trips to South Carolina in late October, 1999 (with permission from my Parole Officer) that I was informed of Lee's impending graduation from the Great Lakes Navy Training Center on November 5, 1999. There was no time for me to return to Colorado and process a new travel permit through my parole officer, so I contacted his office and left a message on the voice mail system that I would be returning to Colorado from my South Carolina trip a couple of weeks late. What I did in actual reality was to drive back to Colorado, and flew out of Colorado Springs to Chicago via Salt Lake City & Louisville/Cincinnati, departing the evening of November 2, 1999 on Delta

Airlines, arriving at Chicago O'Hare the morning of November 3, 1999.

I had made reservations at the Comfort Inn and Suites in Gurnee, Illinois because it was the closest I could get to the Navy Training Center after making my hotel reservations so close to the graduation date. My original reservation was made for November 3 through 6, 1999 (Choice Hotels Central Reservations #78096854) and I extended the reservation directly with the hotel from November 6 through 8, 1999 (Hotel Reservation Confirmation #86467).

I had arrived a day before Lee's Grandmother and Aunt, Delma and Pam Dukes, who were registered at the Red Carpet or Red Roof Inn. After Delma and Pam arrived, I hired the services of Five Star Limousine Service and took them out for a night in Chicago. Delma became tired and after taking her back to her room, Pam and I went out for a while longer. It was on this part of our night out that we were taken to a bar/lounge in the Rush street area. I believe the name of it was "Alibis."

On Friday, November 5, 1999 after attending the ceremony of Lee's graduation from the Great Lakes Navy Training Center in Great Lakes, Illinois, Pam, Delma, and I took Lee and a few of his friends out for a night on the town to celebrate. I again used the services of Five Star Limousine Service. After having a great time about town, we dropped the graduates off on base and Pam and Delma at their motel. As I returned to my hotel, I notified the driver, Jagir Multani, that I would need the car again on Saturday. I also told Multani that there was a chance that Lee would not be able to leave the base, but if that happened, I would still want to go out. We agreed on a pick up time of around six in the evening. Just before returning to the hotel in Gurnee, I asked Mr. Multani if Lee was unable to leave the base, could he find someone who knew Chicago that would be interested in going out and having some fun and show me Chicago. Multani said he had a friend.

On Saturday, November 6, 1999, when Multani called me at the hotel prior to picking me up, I informed him that Lee would not be able to go out and asked if his friend was willing and interested in going out. Multani told me he had spoken to his friend and would call him again.

After picking me up at the hotel, and on the drive into Chicago, Multani made a call from his cell phone. Multani informed me that he had a friend who would be perfect for partying and showing me Chicago. Multani stated the person was a good friend of his and that he, Multani, and this friend had known each other for some time and had done business together. Upon arriving at the lounge, and as he had on the first night out with Five

Star Limo, Multani parked in front and opened the rear door on the driver side. Upon my exiting the limo, I saw a thin built, big eared, light skinned black male dressed preppy standing next to Multani. Multani introduced me to this man as "my friend Barack Obama." When I went to shake Obama's hand and introduce myself, he took my hand and introduced himself as "Barack Obama." It was clear when seeing Multani and Obama interact that both men indeed did clearly know each other well.

Mr. Obama and I had a few drinks and talked for about an hour or so at the bar. I mentioned to him that I could really use a couple of lines to wake up, as I was really tired, but I wanted to do a night on the town while in Chicago. Obama asked if I was referring to coke, and I stated I was. He then told me he could get it for me.

After Obama made a phone call, we left the lounge together in the limo I hired. He instructed the driver as to where we were going. In the limo, I handed Obama two hundred and fifty dollars to pay for an eight ball of cocaine. After what felt like a thirty minute drive, we stopped and Mr. Obama got out of the limo and said he would be right back. He returned after about five minutes had passed, at which time he pulled a packet out of his pocket and handed it to me. I took a CD case I had in the limo with me and put out three lines of cocaine on it. While resting the CD case on Obama's leg and taking a rolled up dollar bill, I snorted one line.

During my conversation with Obama, I had made it very clear that I was openly gay. In my lifetime, I have always been good at judging whether or not a person is interested. My instincts told me that he was. After snorting the first line, I used my right hand to rub Obama's left leg up to his crotch. After he became aroused, I snorted the second line while watching Obama undo his pants and pull out his semi-erect penis. He then began rub-bing his fingers through my hair, then cupping the back of my neck. Obama pulled and pushed me down to his semi-erect penis, and then placed it in my mouth.

As I began to perform oral sex on Obama, I noticed him pulling out another packet from his pocket along with a glass cyl-inder. He then asked to borrow my lighter. As I came up off of Obama's penis to hand him my lighter, I saw him placing a crack cocaine rock in a glass pipe. Obama asked me if I wanted to smoke it, and I informed him "I only snort, I do not smoke it." He then stated that smoking crack makes him harder and hornier longer.

Obama then pushed my face back down into his crotch. I returned to perform oral sex on him while he smoked the crack pipe. After smoking the pipe, Obama began running his fingers through my hair in a soft, sensual manner using his fingertips to trace over the outline of the ridges of my ear, massaging the back of my neck, rubbing my face, holding my head in his hands in the most sensual manner I have ever known. Obama then lit the pipe a second time, and afterwards lowered his pants completely to his ankles, while telling me to suck and lick under his balls and sack.

I continued to perform oral sex on Obama for what seemed like an eternity. When he had his orgasm, he pulled my face up and gently kissed the back of my neck. I laid back and rested against his chest as Obama smoked the pipe a third time. I then did another three lines of coke and stood up out of the sun roof. As I was standing up, the wind blew off a baseball style cap that was given to me by a very dear friend, and I told the driver to pull over. I got out of the limo and ran down the freeway to re-cover my cap. Shortly after recovering my cap and after having a couple more drinks in the limo, we decided to call it a night. It was decided that the driver would take me to my hotel first and then return Obama to his car. I told Obama I really enjoyed my-self, enjoyed meeting him and hoped to be able to visit Chicago and him again soon. Obama told me he enjoyed himself and no one has ever "sucked" him as good in his life.

On Sunday, November 7, 1999, while in my hotel room at the Comfort Inn & Suites in Gurnee, Illinois, I heard a knock on the room door. It was just after the sun had set. When I looked out of the peep hole to see who was knocking, imagine my surprise to find the same man I had been introduced to the evening before, standing outside my hotel room, uninvited and unannounced. I answered the door in anticipation, knowing exactly why he was there. I invited Barack into the room (after what we had done together, I felt I could freely call him Barack) and he immediately pulled out cocaine. I told him I still had some from the eight ball I had purchased from him the night before. Barack then pulled out the same glass pipe he had in the limo the night before and proceeded to smoke a rock of crack cocaine right there in my hotel room.

The visit to my room was a complete surprise to me, and Barack made it clear after lighting his crack pipe that he had come to the hotel for the specific purpose of getting his dick sucked again. In fact, he, himself opened his pants and pulled out his penis. Barack then instructed me to take all of him into my mouth. At this time, he dropped his pants completely to his ankles, and as he lay back on the bed, he instructed me to suck his penis and balls. While sucking Barack's balls, he once again smoked another crack rock.

After bringing him to climax, we laid together for only a couple of minutes, again with Barack kissing on my neck, before he got up, pulled his pants up and left.

On Monday, November 8, 1999, I checked out of the hotel and drove the Mazda 626 rented from Hertz Rent-A-Car back to O'Hare airport and flew back to Colorado. Upon my return to Colorado, I notified my parole officer that I had returned. It was at this time I became aware that during my absence my parole officer had been changed. My newly assigned PO instructed me to report immediately, and I was then placed in the Pueblo County Jail for a little more than a week because as he said, "you do not just leave a message on the answering machine, you need to speak directly with someone to extend your travel permit."

After my release from custody, I continued on with my life. I continued making sales to my childhood friends in South Carolina. On May 5, 2000 (Cinco de Mayo) the Colorado Parole Board discharged my 1986 sentence to the Department of Corrections and did so, some 5 years early.

I did not think much about the two encounters in Chicago, Illinois with the big eared guy who enjoyed smoking crack and getting head. In fact, it was not even until 2004 that I even realized who it was that I had gone down on twice, and who had sold me an eight ball of cocaine.

The Comfort Inn & Suites, Gurnee, Illinois

Where Barack Obama came to get his second blow job and brought more cocaine for me and him….
(Photo from ComfortInn.com)

Lee's Graduation from Basic Trair
The Great Lakes Navy Training Fa

Chapter Four
How I Knew Who I Blew

Most people do not expect to have a two-night stand of quick sex, partying and doing drugs one day and then a few years later seeing the person they went down on, speaking at the Democratic National Convention on television. However, that is exactly what happened to me.

Just under five years later, after performing oral sex on Barack Obama twice and engaging in cocaine use with the man, I ended up staring at him on national television, on air in Mexico of all places. Democrats always said Republicans did this sort of thing. Well, I am a lifelong Democrat and faggot, and it was Barack Obama, the Democrats rising young star that, less than five years earlier, had his dick and nut sack in my mouth, not once, but twice in two days.

It was not until I was watching the 2004 Democratic Convention on Sky Network's coverage (strangely enough) in Nayarit, Mexico that I realized who the crack smoking, big eared Chicago trick was. It was while watching the convention coverage that I sat there looking at Barack Obama on TV and said to myself, "Just like a politician to be smoking crack and having his dick sucked in the shadows."

Even though I realized the man in my limo, and hotel room in 1999 was the non-distinguished Illinois State Senator Barack Obama. You see, I did not live in Illinois nor did I plan to, so confronting such a non-important person over his getting his freak on with a gay white man was not an issue. It did, however, become an issue in 2007. How could it not? After all, this was a man who claimed to be above all the scandal and association of the usual politician and who was running for President of the United States.

It was in September of 2007 that I made what later would be my biggest mistake in holding Barack Obama accountable. You see, I thought I would give Barack Obama the opportunity to acknowledge his adult use of illegal drugs instead of me having to call him a liar publicly. That was probably my biggest mistake and may very well be what got Donald Young killed.

Chapter Five
2007

It was in late August, early September, 2007 that I decided that it was time to contact Barack Obama and request that he publicly correct his lies about the extent of his drug use. I had come to this decision after repeatedly watching coverage on the likes of MSNBC, etc., where the hype about Barack Obama being this "new kind of politics," and this "completely open and transparent candidate" had already started to get old.

I contacted the Obama for America Campaign as well as David Axelrod's AKP Message & Media asking that Barack Obama correct his claims that he has never sold drugs, and that he has "not" used any drugs "since high school." I then explained in detail to the Campaign and to Axelrod's company exactly how I know these statements to be untrue.

In both conversations with Obama for America and AKP Message & Media, I explained that on November 6, 1999, I had been introduced to Barack Obama by a friend and that Obama had, in fact, sold me an eight-ball of cocaine and had himself engaged in smoking crack cocaine in my limo on that date and again in my hotel room the following day. I explained that I had been in the Chicago area for a graduation, and was not asking Obama or his campaign for anything other than that Obama be honest and admit he misspoke about when he had stopped using drugs. It was made clear, by me, to both Obama for America and AKP that Obama was an Illinois State Senator in 1999, was 38 years old (according to his claimed date of birth) and that he was, in fact, procuring and using illegal drugs while employed as an Illinois State Senator.

Eventually, both the Obama for America and AKP said that they would see that Obama was informed, and that I would hear back from them. I had left my cell phone number with the Obama for America office and AKP at that time. In the weeks and months that followed, I left a total of four or five cell phone numbers with the campaign & AKP. The reason for numerous phone numbers was because I changed my cell number to a local number based on where I was living at the time.

Chapter Six

….And In Comes Donald Young

The Death Certificate below is that of Donald Young, Choir Director of Trinity United Church of Christ, 4th Grade School Teacher and by all accounts, a truly caring and warm person….

.

Donald was murdered; shot to death. He was also an openly gay male, by his own admission, and was involved in an intimate and sexual relationship with Senator Barack Obama for years. Donald was killed on December 23, 2007 after having been in communication with me for about four months.

In November 2007, a man by the name of Larry Bland was brutally murdered in Chicago. An openly gay man, Bland would occasionally attend services at Trinity United Christian Church. This coincidentally, is the same church that Barack Obama was a member of for 20 years. Bland, a victim of multiple gunshot wounds, was viciously murdered in his home. Within days of Donald's death, someone started saying the person who murdered Larry Bland in November was the same person that murdered Donald Young in December. Nothing could have been further from the truth.

In fact, the murder of Donald Young was intentionally made to appear similar to the Larry Bland killing in order to trick the police into not looking for the real motive for Donald Young's murder; to silence him. Unlike Larry Bland's apartment, Young's home was not entered by force nor was it robbed. According to Young's roommate, the only items taken from their apartment were small pieces of jewelry. Items that if left behind, could have raised questions as to who might have given them to Donald.

There was a great deal of thought and planning put into the murder of Donald Young. This was essential in making it appear as though the same person had ended Larry Bland's life. Initially, the plan worked, until people close to Donald and his family spoke out accusing the mayor's office and the Chicago police of failing to bring Young's killer to justice. Their inaction was perceived as an obvious attempt to protect the name of Barack Obama. Sadly, the local media assisted the Chicago police with their failure to investigate Donald Young's murder and how Barack Obama was or was not connected to it.

It should be noted that even though Donald Young had not been declared dead until 12:10p.m. Sunday afternoon December 23, 2007; Jeremiah Wright announced Donald's death during at least one early service Sunday morning at Trinity United Church of Christ. Not only did Jeremiah Wright announce Donald's death, he even announced the cause of death, which according to sources would not have been released yet. Jeremiah Wright, just like Barack Obama, already knew Donald Young was dead and how he was killed. Both men also knew who it was that had been chosen to silence Young and protect Barack Obama's bid for the presidency of the United States. Donald was

51

the more likely choice to be killed. After all, if Donald Young began talking, the media would listen to him far more quickly than they would me, because that accuser hadn't lived the colorful life that I had.

According to Donald this communication was at the request of Barack Obama and Pastor Jeremiah Wright. Wright was Obama's spiritual mentor for 20 years while he was a member of the Trinity United Church of Christ where Donald led the choir.

Now imagine this… you are on the road in South Carolina, New Jersey, Pennsylvania, and Delaware looking for a place to relocate, when suddenly you begin receiving phone calls from a man you have never met, do not know and have never spoken to in your life. That is exactly what happened to me.

As stated above, this began shortly after I had contacted 'Obama for America' and 'AKP Message & Media' asking Obama to publicly admit his use of crack cocaine as an adult.

In the early fall of 2007, I received the first phone call from someone claiming to be with the Obama Campaign. It was a man who introduced himself as one, "Mr. Young." This first conversation quickly made it clear that this "Mr. Young" was not responding to my calls representing the Obama Campaign or AKP. You see, "Mr. Young" asked me, "Why didn't you ask

Senator Obama to come clean about the sexual encounters the two of you had in 1999?"

A red flag went up immediately, as I had not mentioned anything to the Obama Campaign or AKP about the sexual encounters; only the drug use. Shortly after this was asked our first conversation ended. It would turn out that the conversations would continue over the next several months, and as they did, "Mr. Young" soon became "Donald Young."

Even as "Mr. Young" became "Donald Young" it still did not dawn on me exactly who this man was other than being someone engaged in a relationship with Barack Obama. After all it was Barack Obama, according to Donald, who had given him my phone numbers, so he could contact me.

Over the course of the next few months, Donald Young confided that Barack Obama himself had asked him to call me and find out who I had spoken to; which media outlets had been contacted; and what reporters, family or friends I had told about the November 1999 encounters between Obama and myself. In these phone conversations and text messages Donald at one point relayed to me, "Barack and his pastor are discussing the best way to publicly correct his statements about the extent of his drug use," leading me to believe that Obama had decided to be honest.

Well, as we all know Obama and Jeremiah Wright never did anything to come clean.

Donald called me again about a week later. In this call, Donald displayed a completely different demeanor specifically when telling me to be careful. Donald stated, "Larry, do not wait for Barack to admit his 1999 drug use. He is not going to admit anything." He then went on to say, "I feel bad that I have been used to get information from you so that Barack and his people can attack you. I realize now that Barack used me to get as much information from you as possible to try and make you look bad." Then he informed me, "You know, Barack and I have been lovers for some time *and* Reverend Wright knows it."

Between September and early December, 2007, Donald Young called me on four (possibly five) different phone numbers. I was moving around a great deal. Donald admitted to me that the numbers were all given to him by Obama. I made sure to update my phone number with Sprint/Nextel/Boost to reflect my current address. With each relocation, I immediately would call the Obama Campaign and tell them the new number, so they would be able to contact me without any problem. The numbers, in fact, were so new that my own mother had not even received them.

With each call Donald became more candid about his phy: interactions with Obama. According to him, he and Barack ha been involved in a sexual relationship for several years and th Reverend Jeremiah Wright, church staff and some members o the congregation knew about it.

During one conversation, Donald informed me that he and Barack engaged in anal intercourse and that Donald had indee penetrated Barack from behind. Donald went even further by saying Barack and he would satisfy each other by "pitching" ; "catching." For those who are not familiar with the terms: "pitching," describes the one who is giving the dick; "catchin the one receiving it.

I *believed* Donald Young, and I also believe that his de: was at the direction of both Barack Obama and Jeremiah Wri On December 27, 2007 just four days after Donald's murder, guy named Joshua posted on a BET message board the follov statement:

"Joshua said on December 27th, 2007 well, I really hope the that he was involved with Obama cannot be linked to this mur der!" http://blogs.bet.com/news/newsyoushouldknow/choir-directoratobama%tp://blogs.bet.com/news/newsyoushouldknc choir-director-atobama%E2%80%99s-church-is-killed/

It was not until late February or early March 2008 that I came to realize the "Mr. Young" contacting me in 2007 was, in fact, the murdered choir director of Trinity United Church of Christ in Chicago. At that time, I immediately began trying to contact the Chicago Police Department investigators handling the Young murder. Not one time did the Chicago police return my calls until the following affidavit dated April 1, 2008 was sent to them. And then they still waited until April 23, 2008, the day after the Pennsylvania primary when Barack Obama was beaten so badly.

Lawrence W. Sinclair
600 West Superior Street
Apt. 604
Duluth, MN 55802
218-464-1113

April 1, 2008

Chicago Police Department
Homicide Investigators
3510 South Michigan Avenue
Chicago, IL 60653

RE: AFFIDAVIT OF LAWRENCE SINCLAIR

To Whom it May Concern:

Attached hereto is a sworn affidavit concerning some contact I had with a gentleman who identified himself to me as one Donald Young of Chicago in the fall of 2007.

I have made several calls to the Chicago Police Department without a single call being returned.

Sincerely,

Lawrence W. Sinclair

AFFIDAVIT OF LAWRENCE W. SINCLAIR

I, Lawrence W. Sinclair do hereby affirm under the penalty of perjury that the following statements are true to the best of my knowledge, and ability and are provided freely to the Chicago IL Police Department.

I, Lawrence W. Sinclair, do state:

1. In September 2007 I contacted the Presidential Campaign of Barack H. Obama, U.S. Senator of IL, to request that Senator Obama publicly correct his stated drug use record to reflect his use of crack cocaine in November 1999.

2. That in making contact I left the Presidential Campaign of Senator Barack H. Obama a contact number for the campaign

*to return my call. The first number provided was a Texas cell
phone.*

*3. That from the period of Labor day weekend 2007
through November 18, 2007 I did provide a total of four (4) different callback numbers to the Obama campaign, as I had moved
and had changed the numbers to reflect locally my place of residence at the time.*

*4. In late September to early October 2007, I received a
call from a male who identified himself as a "Mr. Young" stating
he was calling in regard to calls I had made to the Obama campaign. This first call was, in fact, an attempt by "Mr. Young" to
obtain from me the identities of anyone I had contacted concerning my 1999 allegations against Senator Obama. This first called
shocked me in that this "Mr. Young" asked me why I had not
asked Senator Obama to disclose sexual encounters I had with
Mr. Obama in 1999. I was shocked as I had never mentioned to
the campaign or anyone working for the campaign any sexual
encounters. The call ended with Mr. Young stating I would hear
from someone in a few days.*

*5. In mid to late October 2007, I received a second call
from this "Mr. Young" at which time I clearly became aware that
this individual was personally involved with Senator Obama*

rather than an employee of his campaign, by the tone of the conversation and the sexual nature of said conversation. While "Mr. Young" did not once advise me how he obtained my phone number which by this time had now changed to a Delaware number.

6. In late October 2007 I received a text message from the gentleman identified as "Mr. Young" in which he stated he was intimately involved with Senator Obama and that Obama was discussing with him and his pastor how to publicly acknowledge Senator Obama's drug use in 1999. That Obama wanted to be sure I had not discussed the sexual encounters or drug incident with any media at that time.

7. In mid to late November 2007 another text message from "Mr. Young," but this time to my Minnesota cell phone number, advising me that Obama will publicly correct his statement as to the last time he used drugs, and I did not need to concern myself with publicly disclosing it.

8. The last contact with "Mr. Young" in early December 2007 made it clear to me that Obama had no intentions of publicly acknowledging his 1999 use of crack cocaine and that "Mr. Young" was, in fact, doing nothing more than milking information from me for Senator Obama's use.

9. I had not truly become aware of the murder of Donald Young to the point of understanding this was the individual who had been contacting me last fall until a few weeks ago.

Lawrence W. Sinclair

State of Minnesota }

SUBSCRIBED AND SWORN TO BEFORE ME this day

County of St. Louis }

April 1, 2008 A.D. In the State of Minnesota, County of St. Louis.

The first contact from the Chicago Police Department was a call received on the morning of April 23, 2008 made by a Detective Robert McVicker. My attorney at the time, Montgomery Blair Sibley, returned the call and Det. McVicker and I spoke briefly on the phone. After about two weeks, Det. McVicker asked for the phone numbers on which I had received calls and text messages from Donald Young.

Det. McVicker informed both Mr. Sibley and me that he would obtain the phone records by Grand Jury subpoena directly from the cell phone service provider, which in this case was Sprint/Nextel/Boost. I forwarded the following phone numbers to Det. McVicker through my attorney, Mr. Sibley…956-758-1105; 956-758-1885; 956 758-8002; 302-685-7175; 612-466-1043.

In May, 2008 Obama bloggers claiming to be reporters for the Drudge Report began posting false claims on the internet that the phone numbers provided to the Chicago police had not been active for several years. I called Det. McVicker of the Chicago Police Department who informed me that he had made no such claims and in fact, had not yet received the records from Sprint/ Nextel/Boost stating, "These things do not happen lickety-split." He also stated, "No one in this department has made any statements to anyone as we do not ever comment on ongoing investigations."

Det. McVicker then said, "I did receive one call from a man in Texas claiming to be a reporter for the Drudge Report." I immediately informed him that a man named Scott Covington of Houston, Texas had been stalking, threatening and harassing my mother, my family, my friends and me. As soon as I mentioned the name Covington, Det. McVicker said, "That's him, that's the man that called claiming to be a reporter for the Drudge Report. Larry, I will tell you that no one in my department has made any statements to anyone regarding this investigation. I have received numerous phone calls asking for me, but they refuse to leave their names or call back numbers."

On June 30, 2008, I again called Det. McVicker after a paralegal working for me was told by Sprint/Nextel that they could not provide me with copies of my cell records because they did not exist any longer. Det.McVicker advised me, "I have received the records that I requested from Sprint/Nextel by way of subpoena exactly as I told you I would."

I did not contact the Young family right away as I did not feel it was my place to inform them of this information. However, after the Chicago police were quoted by numerous web sites making disparaging remarks about me, I felt the Young family had the right to be informed of the same things that were provided to the Chicago police. My first contact was with a sister of Donald Young which was limited. I mailed her copies of documents and a letter explaining that I had every reason to believe Barack Obama and Rev. Jeremiah Wright did indeed have Donald murdered. After several months, I felt I owed the Young family the respect to inform them that I was writing this book and provided them the opportunity to express their feelings.

In several telephone conversations with his sisters, brother, nieces and others, I was reassured that the family of Donald Young believed he was murdered to protect Barack Obama. It also became clear, right from the start that members of the Young family were truly fearful of speaking out publicly. To this day, they fear for their own personal, physical safety. In one conversation with a relative, it was expressed that they are one hundred percent convinced if any one of them speaks out publicly on what they believe, they will most certainly be burying another family member at worst, or at least be visiting that person in jail. This family member expressed fear of retaliation by the Chicago police, the Chicago mayor's office, as well as from members and officials of Trinity United Church of Christ. "Larry, you do not understand how things work here in Chicago. My family was put through hell when we accused the mayor's office and the police of covering up Donald's murder," the family member said.

I was told, "Please understand that regardless of what is being said on the internet, we appreciate everything you are doing and have done. Please know that my family is supportive of you, and we are all pulling for you,"

No matter what the Obama people claim or what the Obama bloggers post, the Young family is scared for their lives, and they should not have to live in that kind of fear in the United States of America. The Young family not only knows that Donald was murdered to protect Barack Obama, they also know that no one in Chicago is going to properly investigate or prosecute Donald Young's killer or the individuals who ordered his murder.

At this point in time, the Chicago police have the records from the phone numbers I provided them. What they have done or will do with them is anyone's guess.

Chapter Seven
Going Public

After giving Barack Obama more than four months to publicly announce he misspoke when claiming he had not used drugs since high school, I decided it was time to go public. In the four months that I gave him, he refused to be honest with America. Barack Obama instead decided to play games and use Donald Young to keep me from going public. This whole time, he was planning how to attack me regarding his 1999 crack cocaine use, so I contacted the following news organizations:

- NBC

- CBS

- ABC

- Larry King, CNN

- Anderson Cooper, CNN

- Chris Matthews, MSNBC

- Keith Olbermann, MSNBC

- ➢ Chuck Todd, MSNBC

- ➢ Shepherd Smith, Fox News

- ➢ New York Times

- ➢ New York Post

- ➢ Washington Post

- ➢ Chicago Tribune

- ➢ Los Angeles Times

….and many more.

With all these news organizations, only one contacted me and that was the New York Post.

I was contacted by Jeane McIntosh, a reporter for the New York Post. She told me it was her first priority to determine whether I was for real or just some nut case. In my first conversation with Ms. McIntosh, I informed her "I am not perfect, I have a criminal record, I have served time in Arizona, Florida and Colorado, and I have been involved in moving narcotics and undocumented Mexicans into the United States." She then asked me how I had come to know Barack Obama, and I explained to her how I was introduced to him.

Ms. McIntosh asked what I was trying to get, and I explained I was not looking for anything other than the truth about Barack Obama's drug use to be known. I went on to explain to her that I did not plan on having to expose the sexual encounters, but that I could not just go public with just a part of the story.

Jeane McIntosh and I spoke over the course of a few weeks. During this time, she contacted Citigroup requesting copies of my credit card statement for the period ending November 15, 1999. The request to Citigroup was made to obtain records that would have the exact name of the bar where I was introduced to Barack Obama. Citigroup did contact me after the New York Post request. Citigroup claimed they were searching their archives regarding the requested credit card statement. While Ms. McIntosh was working to obtain the credit card statement from Citigroup, I contacted Choice Hotels for the records from my November 1999 stay at the Comfort Inn & Suites in Gurnee, Illinois.

After several days of working with Jeane McIntosh, I was asked if I would agree to take a polygraph test. I immediately replied "Yes." She informed me that the editors at the New York Post had asked her to ask me about taking a polygraph. Shortly after this request, I began to feel that the editors at the New York Post were taking too long to make up their minds about what they were going to do.

Ms. McIntosh and I continued to work together on the story, but even she started to feel that the Post was dragging its feet. About three days after I was asked if I would agree to a polygraph, Ms. McIntosh informed me that their legal department had come to the conclusion that the New York Post was not going to run the story.

I called Ms. McIntosh and conveyed my feelings to her. It was at this time she told me she too was confused as to what her editors were doing, stating "Larry, I would love to break this story, and I have a lot of time invested in it already. I don't know what they (the editors) are doing, but they keep asking me if I am talking to you and tell me to keep investigating this and then say they aren't ready to print it yet."

Just days before I went public with my January, 2008 YouTube video, I spoke once again with Ms. McIntosh. In this conversation, she told me "Larry, you have given the Post more than enough time to break the story. I just get the feeling they are waiting for someone else to report on it before they go with it. You should not feel bad about going to someone else as you have given the Post more time than anyone I know for the exclusive to the story." It was after that conversation that I decided to record a short video and post it on YouTube. I did stay in contact with Ms. McIntosh after posting the video.

Within two days of posting the less than three minute video on YouTube, I began receiving requests from newspapers and radio shows for interviews. The Chicago Tribune's D.C. reporter, John Crewdson, contacted me through the YouTube page as did New York Times reporter, (Obama hit man) Serge F. Kovaleski, the executive producer of "The Jay Thomas Show" Shawn Kelly, The Jim Sumpter Show, Jeff Rense and many more.

It was on January 23, 2008, that I did my first public interview covering my claims against Barack Obama's crack cocaine use and sexual encounters with me in 1999. That interview was done with Jeff Rense on his radio show. After my first appearance on Jeff's show, I was again contacted by John Crewdson of the Chicago Tribune. At the same time, the Obama Campaign and David Axelrod's ASP Message & Media began its "internet smear campaign" against me.

When Chicago Tribune reporter John Crewdson called my Duluth, Minnesota home asking if I would speak with him, I agreed and also agreed for him to record the conversation. After speaking with Mr. Crewdson several times, I received an email from him the following Monday advising me that he would be arriving in Duluth later that evening.

Mr. Crewdson and I met in person for some five days during the coldest damn week of the year in Duluth. He questioned me on everything from my criminal past, childhood, family, the 1999 Chicago trip, my medical history and more. John asked for and received permission to speak with my mother, the Lee family and anyone else he needed to.

In the course of the five days, I also provided John with my medical records, financial records, phone records; anything he needed to pursue this story. John, in what I believe was meant to secure my trust on the first day, said "Larry, I spoke to David Axelrod (I have known him for twenty-five years) and asked him about your claims. David said he was aware of the claims you have made and he and the Obama camp are currently investigating you and are determined to connect you with the Clinton camp. David says they will destroy you before they allow your claims to see the light of day."

It was after John had completed his interviews, and while we had dinner at Top of the Harbor in Duluth, Minnesota, that John looked at me and said "Larry, tell me right now if you are making this up. If you tell me you are, I will just go home to my family and not ever mention I met with you." I responded "John, I am not making anything up, I am telling you the truth." It was then that John said "If you are telling me the truth, I will do everything I can to print this story. I just don't want you to be fucking with me on this." I assured him I was not. We then left the restaurant and John flew to Chicago trying to track down the limo driver/owner of Five Star. He continued to communicate with me.

During our meetings, John also asked if I would agree to take a polygraph which I agreed to do. Just like the New York Post, he told me that the Tribune's legal department had advised him, they could not pay for the polygraph. John finally called me and said that he was not going to be able to run the story, unless he could speak with the limo driver and stated "Without the driver, there is no story. Even though everything you told me has been verified, without the driver, I cannot prove nor disprove anything."

Interestingly enough, the entire time I was interviewing with Chicago Tribune reporter John Crewdson, the New York Times reporter Serge Kovaleski was emailing and calling two or three times a day asking if I had spoken to any other media. I did not realize it at the time, but Kovaleski wasn't really interested in the story, he was only interested in knowing who I was talking to in the media. Every email and phone call from Mr. Kovaleski always contained the same statement, "Let me know if you get any calls from any other reporters."

While I was holding interviews with John Crewdson of the Chicago Tribune, Kovaleski of the New York Times continued to call me asking what John and I had discussed. He repeatedly stated "You don't want to talk to the Trib, nobody reads them. You want to let the New York Times do your story." There was one call and an email where Kovaleski decided he could dictate to me. At that time, I called him and told him not to call me asking for information. It was as if every reporter or media outlet who contacted me that I informed Kovaleski about, ended up canceling interviews the day after I told him who had contacted me. The Jay Thomas Show was one of those interviews.

Shawn Kelly, the producer for "The Jay Thomas Show" contacted me and scheduled me to go on with Jay Thomas. When I mentioned Serge Kovaleski's name, the show with Jay Thomas was immediately canceled. Shawn Kelly then called me to again schedule my appearance. Less than an hour later, he called again to tell me their legal department is in discussion as to whether I can go on. An hour before I was to go on the show, Mr. Kelly called again to tell me it had been canceled. The media not only knew about my claims, they were more than willing to call me, asking me to do their radio and TV shows, only to back out after it became known I was scheduled to appear on their shows.

Jonathan Roth, Senior Producer of Canadian Televisions "The Standard" not only continued to email and call me, but had arranged for a film crew to set up in my Duluth, Minnesota apartment for an appearance on "The Standard." On Monday night, I had announced I would be appearing on "The Standard" on Wednesday. The next day, Tuesday, I was informed by Mr. Roth that the network was not going to allow the interview.

Now people can say what they want, but it takes money and power to get media outlets to drop interviews and guests from shows within a few hours of airing. It took time and planning to get a film crew arranged and set up in my apartment, only to be called off within hours. Jim Sumpter of the "Jim Sumpter Show", Chris Baker of "Baker in the Morning", Enrique Y Joe in Miami, and other radio hosts found out what the wrath of the Obama Machine would be if they had me on their shows.

What I found even more amazing was the Obama media and its internet allies in their execution of a well organized internet smear campaign, i.e. Dailykos.com, DemocraticUnderground.com, HuffingtonPost.com, diggs.com, and topix.com were all used by the Obama camp to knowingly circulate false statements against me. The Obama Machine claimed I was a patient in a mental hospital in Texas. They circulated retraction letters

which they signed my name to knowing I had not retracted anything.

Eric Gibbons of Bordentown, New Jersey, a disgusting
looking gay artist and owner of Firehouse Gallery, used YouTube
to post claims under the name *tubesocktedd* and Firehouse Gallery, etc.

There came a time when a false letter of apology was circulated by Eric Gibbons aka tubesocktedd/Firehouse Gallery,
zombiekilla, et al, under the supervision and direction of Obama
for America employee Sam Graham Felsen and David Axelrod.
New York Times reporter Serge Kovaleski called to inquire if this
letter was written by me, and I assured him it WAS NOT, yet the
Times allowed it to continue to circulate as true even though the
below letter was never written by me.

Hi,

*This is Larry Sinclair. I am posting this message in venues where
I know my situation is discussed. First off, let me apologize for
the roller coaster ride I have put some of you through (myself included). I have been going through various issues as of late, and
have been having quite a tough time. I sincerely appreciate all the
support I have received from ALL OF YOU (you know who you
are). However, I think it's time this all was finished. I was not be-*

ing honest. I did not give oral sex to Barak Obama, nor have I ever met him. I have just been extremely lonely lately, and I guess I needed attention. I want to assure you, all the money I received from this (both from Whitehouse.com and The Globe Magazine) will ALL go to charity. When all is said and done, I will NOT HAVE PROFITED from this. Now that I have disclosed this, I hope you all will respect my right to privacy, and let it rest. I have made some good friends during this, and will always cherish and respect the ones who have helped me.

Thank you,

Larry Sinclair

On February 21, 2008, a fake Washington Post Editorial, page 1a2, contained the following which was written and distributed by the Obama for America internet network bloggers under the supervision of paid campaign employee Sam Graham Felsen and David Axelrod.

"In late fall of 2007 Lawrence Sinclair approached campaign officials of the Sen. Barack Obama campaign, and told them a very disturbing story. Rob Allen of the Sen. Obama campaign stated. After the meeting had concluded the campaign officials ruled it off, as "just someone trying to make a buck."

The following week they received a phone call, from a man claiming to represent Mr. Sinclair, and demanding $100,000.00 as restitution for his client.

Lawrence Sinclair has filed a federal suit against Barack Obama and others for harassment since the gay man released his video on YouTube.com, an internet web-site for viewing homemade videos, alleging that, the Senator from Illinois and Mr. Sinclair shared oral sex and cocaine in the back of a Mr. Sinclair's limo in Gurnee, IL in 1999.
mzmolly *(1000+ posts)   Mon. Feb-25-08 03:15 PM*

Original message

Larry Sinclair - Lies about Obama - Documented

Edited on Mon Feb-25-08 03:21 PM by mzmolly

Additionally, I found a Larry Sinclair from Texas who contributed to the Bush Campaign and the Republican Party in 1989.

1. Larry Sinclair is a Ron Paul supporter, DIGGS.COM.

2. Larry Sinclair is a mental patient who was institutionalized in 1999 on the date he claims to have had the "encounter" with Obama.

I know that no one here believes this nonsense, but I wanted to share regardless.

Everything stated above by Denise Lee, aka MzMolly of DemocraticUnderground.com is completely false, and she knew before publishing them that they were outright lies. Sam Graham-Felsen and Nate Green, both paid by Obama for America, knowingly posted false statements calling me a wanted pedophile and posted fake Washington Post articles claiming I had attempted to blackmail other politicians.

At this time, Obama's "go to guy" David Axelrod was trying hard to live up to his statement to Chicago Tribune Reporter John Crewdson, saying "We will destroy him". Axelrod soon realized I'd fight back, and he needed more than his internet lies. He found what he thought was his game-over play. He found internet porn punk Dan Parisi and his sidekick Robert Braddock of Charlotte, North Carolina.

On February 11, 2008, I filed a pro-se Civil Action in the U.S. District Court of Minnesota against Barack Obama, David Axelrod and the Democratic National Committee.

Jeane McIntosh of the New York Post was immediately instructed to write the story and have it in by press time. On February 12, 2008, I was informed by Jeane that she had written the story and turned it into her editor, and it was believed by both Jeane and I, that the story would appear in the February 13, 2008 issue of the New York Post.

That was not to be the case. However, as Jeane informed me that after she was ordered to have the story written and turned in that day, a political editor for the New York Post killed it at the last minute. Jeane said "Larry, I don't know what to think at this point, especially after being ordered to have the story turned in first thing, and then it gets killed."

That same week, internet pornography producer Dan Parisi of Whitehouse.com came out of nowhere and published a challenge on his website to arrange a polygraph test paid for by Whitehouse.com. This is where the Dan Parisi and David Axelrod polygraph scam began.

WhiteHouse.com's Saturday delivered offer.

Chapter Eight
Parisi/Axelrod Polygraph Scam

On February 13, 2008, I called former FBI polygraph expert Jack Trimacarco to inquire as to what it would cost me to have a polygraph administered. I left Mr. Trimacarco a voice message explaining I was looking for an "apolitical, objective and impartial polygraph expert" to administer a polygraph exam of me on my claims about Barack Obama. On Valentine's Day of 2008, I posted on my YouTube page that I was trying to arrange a polygraph exam. The next day, on February 15, 2008, I received an email asking me "Larry, are you going to accept the $100,000 offer from Whitehouse.com?" Needless to say, I had no idea what this person was talking about, and I informed them of this.

In a second email, I was informed that the website Whitehouse.com had published a "$100,000 polygraph challenge" and they included a link to their site. Before this, I had never heard of nor had I visited Whitehouse.com, which I later found out was in fact an internet pornography site up until January, 2008… January, 2008 being the month my public YouTube announcement was posted. The Whitehouse.com website reads as follows:

Whitehouse.com Presents: The $100,000 Larry Sinclair Poly-

graph Challenge....

2/15/08 3:30 PM

Alright, Larry Sinclair, we have seen your video saying you had a couple of hot nights with Barack Obama. You "performed oral sex" on him while he smoked crack a few years back in Illinois.

It's a pretty good story, but we have to admit that it sounds a bit far-fetched. Please pardon us for being skeptical though Larry, it's just these crazy times we live in.

However, we're glad you said you'd be willing to take a polygraph test – we want to pay you to take one. $10,000 to be exact, just for taking the test, regardless of the result. You get the money, we get to make a video of the whole things, and it's a deal.

Furthermore, Larry, buddy, if you happen to pass the test, we'll give you ten times that amount: $100,000. We'll even pay for your airfare and two nights in a hotel.

That's our offer – we've posted it here on the site and make sure you watch your mail Larry; we've already sent you a contract – signed, sealed (and soon to be) delivered by Federal Express.

A hundred grand from us to you if you're telling the truth or ten grand just for being a good sport if it turns out you're totally full of it. We think that's more than fair. Like you said," America deserves to know. As we say, either put up or shut up."

On Saturday, February 16, 2008 I received via FedEx a one page document from Dan Parisi, founder and owner of Whitehouse.com, the document stated as follows:

Whitehouse.com Inc.
209 Greenwich Street
Suite 194
New York, New York 10006

2/15/08

Dear Mr. Sinclair:

We have seen your video that you have made in regard to your relationship with Mr. Barack Obama. We are offering you $10,000 to just show up within the next 10 days and take a multi-questioned polygraph test administered by a professional at our offices which will be videotaped and broadcasted. We will also have to be the first and only entity that you will be taking a polygraph test with on this matter in the past or over the next four weeks. We will get and pay for your airfare and two nights at a hotel while you are here at our offices, and you will be paid the $10,000 at the end of the test. If you successfully pass the polygraph test, and it shows that you are telling the truth and you indeed did drugs with Senator Obama and had sex with Senator Obama, we will pay you an additional $90,000. Please respond to me by email at dparisi@ Whitehouse.com by February 21, 2008 to accept the offer, or it will expire.

Very truly yours,

Dan Parisi
President

Upon receiving the written document above, I contacted Dan Parisi of Whitehouse.com, who had increased his website traffic by 3,000% with his offer. This is where the Dan Parisi and David Axelrod polygraph scam began.

In my contact with Dan Parisi, I informed him there would be conditions Whitehouse.com had to meet for me to consider accepting his offer. Those conditions included:

1.   Whitehouse.com and Dan Parisi must provide sworn statements they are not involved with any Presidential candidate, a candidate's campaign, nor representing anyone associated with any candidate or their campaign;

2.   I must be allowed to know what polygraph examiners are chosen, and I must agree to these being selected;

3.   I must be allowed to have at least one member of the media of my choice to be present and witness the entire examination;

4.   The polygraph examiner must tell Dan Parisi and me at the same time the results of the polygraph;

5.   Parisi and Whitehouse.com must pay all expenses associated including but not limited to airfare, ground transportation, hotel, food, etc.;

6.   That I be provided copies of all polygraph exam data and video;

7.   That all results will be announced by both parties (Whitehouse.com and Larry Sinclair) at the exact same time and date.

Dan Parisi of Whitehouse.com responded by email accepting all of my conditions, yet immediately began violating them.

First Parisi failed to provide the required sworn statement and instead posted a half-ass disclaimer on his Whitehouse.com site, saying he did not know any of the candidates and had never spoken to them.

Secondly, Parisi knowingly caused my choice for examiner, Jack Trimarco, to decline my request on February 17, 2008, one day after agreeing that I had a say as to who would be chosen. After Trimarco was eliminated from the pool, Parisi notified me that *he* had chosen Edward I. Gelb, and had already scheduled it with Gelb's Los Angeles office.

After being informed by Whitehouse.com, they had secured Ed Gelb, I notified the Chicago Tribune Reporter, John Crewdson, and asked if he would be my independent media witness. Mr. Crewdson contacted Edward Gelb's office to question whether, in Gelb's opinion, my medical conditions and medications would affect the polygraph results. Within five minutes of Crewdson's phone call to Edward Gelb's office, I received three calls from Dan Parisi's assistant, Robert Braddock, asking "why did you tell Crewdson we were using Gelb? Please inform Crewdson he cannot call or question Gelb anymore." So the agreement for an independent media witness was being reneged on now.

On the day I was to fly out to Los Angeles, Parisi posted on his site that I had asked to change the payment terms. This was an outright lie by Parisi and on the morning of February 21, 2008, he suggested a "flat fee" to avoid legal questions. After Parisi suggested the change in terms, I agreed with conditions; those being $10,000 to charity, which to this date has yet to be paid. Parisi's deliberate and calculated misrepresentations, raised flags concerning his intent.

Whitehouse.com had stated a limo would pick me up and take me to the airport. Instead, Parisi's assistant Braddock escorted me like a prison guard from my home to Los Angeles.

Upon my arrival in Los Angeles, the so-called ground transportation was nowhere to be found. The hotel did not have the reservation and Parisi tried to prevent me from having dinner after finally getting checked into the Hilton Checkers Hotel. Needless to say, all of the agreed upon conditions for the Whitehouse.com polygraph challenge had been totally disregarded and denied by Dan Parisi.

On Friday, February 22, 2008, Dan Parisi, a short hump-backed man with pop bottle glasses, pulled up in front of the Hilton in a rental Mustang. His appearance reminded me of the old pervert sitting in a *25cent* adult video arcade playing with himself. What I did not know until later was that Parisi and his assistant Braddock had just returned from a pre-exam meeting with Edward I. Gelb (the fake Ph.D.) polygraph examiner.

After picking up something from his room, Parisi returned and he, Braddock, and I drove to the offices of Edward Gelb located at 4201 Wilshire Boulevard, #312, Los Angeles, CA. On the drive to the office of Gelb, Parisi began demanding that I turn over all receipts and the limo driver's name to him. I informed Mr. Parisi that was not part of our agreement, and I would not do that. Right at that moment, I received a call from Jerome Corsi, but was being told by Parisi and Braddock that I needed to hang up. I received a second call from Corsi as we drove into the parking lot at Gelb's office and Parisi's assistant, Rob Braddock, grabbed my phone and hung up.

After arriving in the office of Edward Gelb, I immediately started to sense the entire thing was a setup. First, Edward Gelb, Dan Parisi and his assistant, Rob Braddock, spent close to two (2) hours in Gelb's office, behind closed doors. Finally, Edward Gelb comes into the reception area and introduced himself. It was at this time that Parisi walked by and Gelb asked him if the receptionist had informed him of "the additional cost for your request." Parisi responded "she had, and I gave her a check for the additional costs".

After sitting in the waiting area for about two hours while Gelb, Parisi and Braddock discussed *whatever* behind closed doors, Mr. Gelb came out of his office to the waiting area. He then asked me to accompany him to the restroom to provide a urine sample for a drug screen. What makes this highly unusual is that another man awaiting a polygraph in Gelb's office was escorted by an office employee to provide the urine sample. Simply stated, Edward Gelb does not routinely escort people to the bathroom to watch them piss!

After returning from the bathroom, I again was told to wait while Gelb, Parisi, and Parisi's assistant Braddock, continue their private pow-wow. After finally being called into Gelb's office, it became clear to me this was not meant to be a simple polygraph. Edward Gelb had turned over total control to Dan Parisi and when Parisi and Braddock finally left the office, it was quickly made clear this "polygraph" was actually a fishing trip.

Edward Gelb from the very beginning lied through his teeth. Gelb claimed he needed to conduct a Q&A to determine what questions to ask once the polygraph began. Immediately, Gelb started his Q&A by asking about my family; their names, ages, birth dates, where they lived, married or not, where they worked, etc. None of which had anything to do with Barack Obama engaging in sexual acts with me and/or Barack Obama's smoking of crack cocaine and his selling me an eight ball of cocaine. The questions continued about whom in my family had been informed of my allegations about Barack Obama and whether or not these family members had anything to do with me making the allegations.

After spending what felt like an unreasonable amount of time questioning me about my family, Gelb then switched to questions about who in the media I had spoken to, what news organizations they worked for, what their responses were etc, etc. Gelb was fixated on finding out every detail about my conversations with New York Post reporter Jeane McIntosh and Chicago

Tribune Reporter John Crewdson. When it came to the New York Times Reporter Serge Kovaleski, Gelb showed no interest what-so-ever in what was said to Kovaleski. After continuing his questioning about who I had contacted in the media, and what I had told them, Gelb starts asking about where I had worked and lived.

Even though I had stopped Gelb and asked him point blank why he wanted all this information about me, my family, who I had spoken within the media etc, Gelb continued with this line of questioning for another two plus hours claiming it was necessary to form a list of questions to ask me once the polygraph exam began. Well, I had taken a polygraph some years earlier and Gelb's answer did not make any sense because my previous polygraph did not entail any such "fishing expedition". In fact, after almost four hours of questioning about everything short of what color my last bowel movement was, when Gelb was ready to tell me the questions that would be asked once I was connected to the polygraph machine, he simply reached across his desk and picked up a single page that had the polygraph questions already typed out in color ink.

After more than five plus hours the process was complete and Dan Parisi and Robert Braddock entered Gelb's office. They asked me and Gelb to sit there looking like we were engaged in the polygraph so Braddock could take some pictures for posting on Whitehouse.com. In other words, the photos published on Whitehouse.com claiming to be of me taking the polygraph were fakes. The cable across my chest was not connected and was held in place by me squeezing my left arm against my side to keep it from falling down.

It became perfectly clear to me that the polygraph exam was rigged even before leaving the offices of Edward Gelb. Before leaving, standing with Edward Gelb, Dan Parisi and Parisi's assistant Robert Braddock, I specifically asked Gelb, "Well, what's the result? Am I telling the truth or not?" Simultaneously Gelb and Parisi assistant Robert Braddock responded, *"We will not know until Monday after the results are reviewed by another examiner."* You see, I knew this was not true because as I said, I had taken a polygraph before and the results were known immediately.

Even after Gelb and Parisi assistant Robert Braddock had both stated that the results would not be known until the following Monday, February 25, 2008, I began receiving demanding, threatening calls from both Parisi and his assistant Robert Braddock the very next day, Saturday, while traveling back to Duluth, Minnesota. Braddock and Parisi left repeated voice mails on Saturday, February 23, 2008 demanding that I provide them the name of the limo driver, making out-right false claims that I had agreed to give them that information and even claimed that I had already provided that information to reporters, when, in fact, I had not promised them any such information nor had I provided it to any reporter. In addition to demands for the name of the limo driver, Parisi's assistant Robert Braddock demanded copies of emails between me and Attorney Gloria Allred, saying that they had the right to have proof that I had been in contact with Ms. Allred. I refused to provide those emails to Braddock who responded by saying that if I did not provide him and Parisi with the name of the limo driver and copies of emails between me and Attorney Allred by five that afternoon, Whitehouse.com was prepared to publish that I had failed the polygraph. These threats continued until Sunday, February 24, 2008 when Braddock and Parisi emailed and telephoned me claiming they were publishing that the results showed I was lying.

Throughout the day Sunday Braddock and Parisi claimed they had the polygraph report and were emailing it to me. When they failed to do that they claimed it would be faxed within fifteen minutes, and then when they failed to do that, they claimed they had a hand-written report and were awaiting the type-written report which was finally provided more than five hours later. What is very telling in this so called report (claiming I failed the polygraph) is none other than Edward I. Gelb's own words and date that he claims his findings were determined.

Gelb, on Friday, February 22, 2008 point blank stated the polygraph results would not be known until Monday. Then Gelb issued two pages claiming to be reports from "two" separate polygraph exams, resulting in "deception found." What one should pay very close attention to in Gelb's minimal reports are the following:

1. Gelb's report is dated February 22, 2008, the very date he claimed the results would not be known until the following Monday, or February 25, 2008.

2. The very last line of Gelb's reports: "The polygraphs were "blind scored" by another expert examiner who independently corroborated the findings of the primary examiner."

Well, Edward Gelb perjured himself in making this claim on February 22, 2008, as is clearly demonstrated by the report of Salt Lake City, Utah polygraph examiner Gordon Barland, who was the "other expert examiner" chosen by Dan Parisi (without any prior knowledge by me, even though Parisi claimed I had approved both experts). You see, Barland clearly stated in his report (which Parisi and Whitehouse.com never published), that he could not conduct a "blind" study of the examination due to

Gelb's releasing his findings prior to Barland having received the data to be reviewed. Gordon Barland's review was not conducted until Tuesday, February 26, 2008, yet Gelb stated on February 22, 2008, the "blind score" had already been conducted.

The polygrams were "blind scored" by another expert examiner who independently corroborated the findings of the primary examiner.

Edwan d. Gelb

Edward I. Gelb   CPE (Certified Polygraph Examiner)
PCA Examiner
Past President, American Polygraph Association

In fact, at 12:48 a.m. on February 25, 2008 (the day before Barland's review was even conducted), I received a telephone tip from 207-252-2796 and 207-899-0872, advising me that the polygraph was rigged and was arranged by Dan Parisi and Obama Campaign advisor David Axelrod. The man giving me the tip stated that, "Axelrod and the Obama campaign had agreed to pay Dan Parisi of Whitehouse.com, $750,000 to arrange a rigged polygraph. Parisi and Axelrod were in a heated argument because the Obama camp wanted Parisi to publish that you had failed the polygraph faster than what Parisi had said. Parisi was refusing to publish anything further on the polygraph until he was paid the other half of the three-quarters of a million dollars agreed on."

When I received this information, I contacted Dan Parisi and informed him of what was stated, and I asked Parisi to confirm or deny the allegations. Instead of Parisi denying or confirming the allegations that he refused to respond to the statements and then posted a statement on Whitehouse.com that he had been threatened repeatedly by "Sinclair's supporters and that Whitehouse.com would not publish anything further regarding Larry Sinclair." In addition, Parisi immediately shut down Whitehouse.com, completely scrubbed the site of all posts and comments on the Larry Sinclair/Barack Obama story, and revamped the format of the website requiring individuals to register with Whitehouse.com before being able to comment. It was at that time, Whitehouse.com became the staunchest promoters of Barack Obama, while slamming Hillary Clinton non-stop. I also had asked Parisi to respond; I forwarded the information to Chicago Tribune reporter John Crewdson and asked him to look into who the tipster was. Crewdson actually spoke to the tipster and was told the same thing. In addition, the tipster stated that I should look very carefully at the FEC campaign finance reports for the period from January 1 through March 31, 2008 for the payments to Parisi. The tipster also advised me that Parisi had many different holding companies, and the Obama campaign would not have made a single individual payment.

Immediately after confronting Whitehouse.com's Dan Parisi about the allegations that he arranged a rigged polygraph exam, he issued a stop payment of the check issued to me for the polygraph exam. You see, Parisi had made a deal with David Axelrod and the Obama campaign. All of this occurred on the very day that I published emails to Mr. Parisi asking for his response to the claims made in an anonymous telephone tip.

The Obama campaign, supporters, surrogates, MSNBC's Keith Olbermann, Dailykos.com, etc. immediately saturated the internet with posts that I had failed the polygraph based on the reports of Edward Gelb. What they did not report is that Edward Gelb lied on his reports when he claimed his findings had already been corroborated by the "blind score" that Gordon Barland did not conduct until February 26, 2008; four days after the date of Gelb's claims! Also, not reported was that Edward Gelb, who has a history of always issuing detailed examination reports, including the computer scoring, chose not to issue these reports in regard to this polygraph. They also did not report that the computer analysis of the polygraph contradicted Gelb's findings and found me to be telling the truth, with the possibility of deception at 0.001. In layman's terms, the computer found that I was telling the truth.

The following is one of several polygraph expert's opinion, who also questioned the results and the way the polygraph was even administered by Edward Ira Gelb.

Dear Mr. Sinclair,

I'll be happy to give Mr. Sibley a call on Tuesday. But, perhaps it's best if I provide you with a written summary of my opinion regarding the polygraph examination arranged by White-house.com.

For full disclosure, let me state up front that I support Barack Obama's candidacy for president of the United States and have contributed to his campaign.

1) Firstly, it's important to understand that while there is a widespread public belief in the polygraph, the consensus view among scientists is that it's junk science. Even under the best conditions, lie detector testing still has no scientific basis and the results are not to be relied upon. I suspect that many who cite your polygraph results to discredit you would instead be discrediting the polygraph had Ed Gelb proclaimed you truthful. It's important to understand that polygraph results are not evidence, one way or another.

2) The manner in which Gelb's polygraph examination of you was conducted raises special concerns. We know from his polygraph

report for Wendy Ellis, the former prostitute whom Gelb poly-
graph regarding her claim that U.S. Senator David Vitter was a
client, that Gelb has previously included computerized scoring
results in his polygraph reports. But, in your case, Gelb, for some
reason, failed to mention the computerized results. Thanks to
Gordon Barland's review, we know that on the drug question, you
received the same computerized score as Wendy Ellis did: less
than a 1% probability of deception. That's about as high a pass-
ing score as one can possibly attain. Neither Gelb nor Barland
have provided an adequate explanation, of how they arrived at
their hand scored results completely contradicting the computer-
ized result.

3) We don't know what the computerized scoring results were for
the sex question, as Mr. Gelb did not provide the raw data to Dr.
Barland for analysis.

4) As Antipolygraph.org has documented (http://
antipolygraph.org/articles/article-036), Ed Gelb, who conducted
your polygraph examination, is fraudulently passing himself off
as a Ph.D. in marketing his services to the public. His academic
fakery does not speak well of his credibility. It's hard to think of a
good faith reason why Whitehouse.com would have selected this
polygraph operator to examine you. Had Dan Parisi done due

diligence by simply Googling Ed Gelb's name, he would have
learned of this ethical cloud hanging over Gelb's head.

5) Whitehouse.com failure to fulfill its promise to make publicly
available the video of your polygraph examination raises further
questions, suggesting that there may be something about the con-
duct of the examination that it does not want to be publicly
known.

Sincerely,
George W. Maschke, Ph.D.
Antipolygraph.org
Voice Mail/Fax: 1-206-600-5859
PGP Public Key: 0x74DE6533
AOL Messenger: GeorgeMaschke
Skype (Internet Phone/Text Chat): georgemaschke
Gizmo (secured with Zfone): georgemaschke

Chapter Nine

Obama for America Attacks

Even before the polygraph exam had begun, members of the Obama for America campaign had already started attacking me. An Austin, Texas man named Paul Tarlow quickly registered the domain name LarrySinclair.com. Tarlow told a Washington, D.C. political website the act was a "small contribution to the Obama campaign."

Obama Supporter Buys LarrySinclair.com

Friday, February 22nd, 2008 11:29 AM by BHDC Staff
Filed under: Sex, Scandals, Scoops, Bill O'Reilly, Barack Obama, Larry Sinclair, Paul Tarlow

Barack Obama *supporter* **Paul Tarlow**, *owner of a kiln-formed glass studio in Austin, Texas, has purchased and registered the domain name LarrySinclair.com in an attempt to diffuse allegations of the brewing   drug use and sexual encounter controversy that has erupted on YouTube and been briefly alluded to on air by* **Bill O'Reilly**.

The site claims that **Larry Sinclair** *is using his newly found fame to harm the Obama campaign and benefit financially.*

Tarlow told **Big Head DC** *that he* "**picked up the domain to keep it out of general circulation — a small contribution to the Obama campaign**". *He added that he has no plans to sell the domain name.*

Tarlow, an Austin, Texas kiln-formed glass dealer and Obama supporter, then posted a statement at *LarrySinclair.com* calling me a liar. Mr. Tarlow had never met me, and I knew nothing about him, other than he was an Obama for America internet thug.

After the polygraph exam was announced by the internet pornography fraud Dan Parisi on Whitehouse.com, the website MyBarackObama.com (operated by Obama for America), went crazy attacking me and arguing that polygraph exams are not admissible and are not reliable. In fact, prior to the announcement of the alleged failure of the exam, the Obama machine had saturated the internet with knowingly false stories and accusations, that I was a certified psychotic who had been held in a locked mental hospital for years (even going as far as to say I was in a mental hospital in Texas in November 1999 when I was not). They also made the claim that mental patients could lie and still be found by a polygraph to be telling the truth. MyBarackObama.com even started a Wikipedia page, specifically intent on attacking me and published outright false information about me that was portrayed by Wikipedia as factual. When the connection between the Wikipedia page and the Obama camp became public, the Obama camp immediately scrubbed its Obama for America and My-BarackObama.com websites from Wikipedia.

The information Edward Gelb had obtained from the extensive pre-polygraph interview suddenly was being posted on the internet at DemocraticUnderground.com, MyBarackObama.com, HuffingtonPost.com and others. Only the information had been distorted and edited. In fact, it was after the rigged "polygraph/ fishing expedition" arranged by Dan Parisi in a deal with advisor David Axelrod, that direct attacks began on the internet and by phone against my father's last wife, my nieces and nephews, my mother and my brothers and sisters.

After the fall out between Whitehouse.com's Dan Parisi and Obama campaign adviser David Axelrod resulted in White-house.com pulling back from continuing its polygraph fraud, the Obama campaign began circulating faked retraction letters they claimed to be from me. One letter was even sent to the New York Times, which to my surprise went the extra mile, and had Times reporter Serge Kovaleski call me and ask if the retraction was written by me or not. Of course it was not, but did the Times bother to report the Obama camp had intentionally and deliberately sent them a forged retraction from Obama's accuser? No, they did not. In fact, after the retraction letter failed, Obama media spokesmen Robert Gibbs and Bill Burton decided to start circulating statements via the internet claiming that I had, along with another individual, attempted to extort the Obama campaign out of $100,000. Not only did the Obama camp outright lie about the alleged extortion attempt, they went even further by circulating a fake statement claiming "Larry Sinclair has been investigated eight times in 25 years for blackmail, including black politicians in Indiana and Illinois."

Then the Obama camp claimed that I was a lifelong drug addict who engaged in prostitution in exchange for drugs. I think when the Obama team started circulating this claim; they were really talking about their own candidate's activities on the South-side of Chicago, at Columbia University and in Hawaii. The attacks would persist and have continued to this day. Old bad check charges from Florida that were dismissed in 1986 after I was sentenced in Colorado, suddenly popped back up on sheriff's department's sites. Obama bloggers began publishing claims that I was hiding from a 1986 Pasco County, Florida warrant which was dismissed in 1986 when Florida officials were bound by law to either prosecute me or remove the charges. How this old 1986 charge resurfaced is anyone's guess, but it never once surfaced in any criminal check by any law enforcement agency including the U.S. Department of Justice in more than twenty years. I contacted Pasco County Florida Assistant State Attorney Manny Garcia and the matter was taken care of by simply paying the value of the check (which was cheaper than my traveling to Florida from

104

Minnesota to have a judge dismiss it, but the charge was dropped by the State Attorney's office).

The Obama camp started to realize that no matter what they claimed and spread about me on the internet, I was not going to shut up nor was I going away. I had filed a suit against three bloggers who knowingly published the false information circulated by the Obama campaign in an effort to slander and libel me. The U.S. District Court Judge for the District of Columbia granted a motion for limited discovery from Google/YouTube, DemocraticUnderground.com, Diggs.com and some anonymous bloggers who claimed they could not afford legal counsel. All of a sudden these idiots were being represented by "Obama friendly" attorneys from Ray Beckerman to Paul Allen Levy of Public Citizens Litigation Group (Levy engaged in threats, intimidation, harassment, and illegally obtaining and releasing private records on the internet assisted by Obama for America). All of these attorneys were retained at the request of Obama for America. They fought to protect the identities of the bloggers because revealing their names would most certainly expose Obama for America, David Axelrod, Bill Burton, Robert Gibbs, David Plouffe, and their association with the bloggers and the false information they continued to publish attacking me.

The attacks began to spread to my attorney, Montgomery

Blair Sibley, and were led by Paul Allen Levy and the Obama camp. The D.C. Bar counsel was pressured into moving to revoke Sibley's ability to practice law in the District of Columbia. In fact, a Burlington, Massachusetts woman by the name of Ruth Ellen Kessler (an Obama blogger using the screen name, "Demacratista") publicly posted on the internet how she was involved in assisting Paul Levy of Public Citizens Litigation Group and the D.C. law firm of Klamaski & Associates; ensuring that Montgomery Blair Sibley would not be allowed to represent me in the civil suit against the bloggers Tubesocktedd, MzMolly and OwningLiars, who she claimed were friends of hers. Ruth Ellen Kessler actually engaged in fraud by providing my Social Security number to individuals for the express intent to use it for illegal purposes. Kessler, by the way, turned out to be associated with MyBarackObama.com, Jews for Obama and The Obama Brigade. Ruth Kessler, joined by Houston, Texas con man Scott and Laurie Covington and Lawrenceville, Georgia resident Sheila Bryant, began a continuing criminal enterprise of harassment, threats, fraud, internet hacking, theft of private emails and illegal use of my Social Security number; all in attempts to protect Barack Obama from ever having to be confronted with any questions about his own actions. The entire purpose was to engage me in an internet war to make me look as if I was some unstable psycho so the media would simply ignore the truth. These individuals under the full assistance, cooperation, knowledge and funding of Obama for America, repeatedly posted claims accusing me of being a pedophile, rapist, mental patient, etc. To this day, the Obama camp continues to make these false claims in an ongoing effort to shame anyone in the media from confronting Barack Obama about the fact that he is a closet homosexual, or that he sold cocaine while an Illinois State Senator. And that Obama smoked crack cocaine as recently as November 1999, if not more recently.

To this very day, the attacks continue. From the IRS reviewing my tax returns (even though by law I am not even required to file), to false reports having been repeatedly made to Social Security claiming I have received hundreds of thousands of dollars and that my disability is fraudulent (it was Social Security doctors who did the medical determination on my disability). Furthermore, there are reports to the U.S. Postal Service falsely alleging mail fraud for no other reason than to keep me neck deep in investigations, so I cannot get this book out.

The following are just a few of the outright lies circulated on the internet by Robert Gibbs, Bill Burton and David Axelrod of the Obama for America campaign. The first lie listed below claims that I released my medical records at the June 18, 2008 National Press Club press conference, when NO medicals records were ever released then, or at any other time.

There were huge sections of Larry Sinclair's medical reports (which he provided at his June press conference) which were blacked out. My source purported to have obtained an unedited version of his medical reports which indicate that Sinclair has been HIV positive since 2000. Seeing as there is a lag time between HIV being contracted and when it can appear in testable levels, the implication was that Barack Obama himself may have contracted AIDS from his (alleged) encounter with Sinclair in 1999.

The next one was circulated by Nate Green of My-BarackObama.com, a paid blogger of the Obama for America campaign under the supervision of David Axelrod and Bill Burton.

The man in the tape is a mental patient who wasn't in Chicago in November 1999 because he was in a mental institution. (Written By Nate: February 13, 2008 11:42am)

In addition, this one, a couple of days after the Obama camp first started circulating the lie claiming I was in a mental institution. The Obama camp even claimed that the November 5, 1999 Naval Basic Training Graduation did not take place, yet Great

Lakes Navy Training Center records show it did, and in fact, graduates a class every Friday at the facility.

A reporter in Chicago did his research and found that this man was in a mental institution at the time he specified. Not only that,, but the graduation he mentioned, took place two weeks before the date he mentions. Keep in mind that an insane man would pass a polygraph test, because he would really believe it happened. (Written By Renegade February 15, 2008 @11:13pm)

It seems Nate and Renegade did not do their homework, not to mention that they failed to identify this so called "Chicago Reporter." In fact, Chicago Tribune Reporter John Crewdson had already verified I indeed was in the Chicago area during the period stated of November 3, 1999 through November 8, 1999, and that I did attend the Basic Training Graduation at the Great Lakes Navy Training Center on November 5, 1999 exactly as I had stated.

Kerrie Lanigan
Senior Paralegal

March 27, 2008

VIA FEDERAL EXPRESS

Larry Sinclair
600 W Superior Street
Apt. 604
Duluth, MN 55802

Re: **Stay Information for Larry Sinclair**

Dear Mr. Sinclair:

Your request for information regarding your stay at a Choice branded property has been forwarded to me for response.

While I cannot authenticate any information you currently have in your possession, I have attached copies of the information that has been generated by our system with regard to the stay information you requested.

Very truly yours,
CHOICE HOTELS INTERNATIONAL, INC.

Kerrie Lanigan
Senior Paralegal

110

Stay Details for LARRY SINCLAIR

Property	Hotel Name	Hotel City		
LL142	COMFORT SUITES	GURNEE		

Stay Type	Stay Status	CRS Conf #	PMS Conf #	Cancellation #	Reservation Source
	Checked Out		86467		

Folio					
Room Type	Payment Method	DOA	LOS	# Rooms	Res. Booked Date	Source of Stay
HTSH		11/06/99	2	1		Property

Hotel Room Rev	Award Eligible Rev	Currency Exchange Rate	Award Revenue	Total Award
148.00 USD	148.00 USD	1.000000 USD per USD	148.00 USD	1480.00 pts

Expected TAI Date	CRS Hotel TAI Date	SRP Code	Denial	Invoice Property	Trans Date
04/13/00		SCR	N	Y	04/10/00

Non-qual Reason   Entry ID

Transaction Details

Promo Code	Description	Award Amount
CUS	US COMFORT HOTELS BASIC STAY	1480.00 pts

US COMFORT HOTELS BASIC STAY

http://prodcisapp.choicl.com:8000/cis/servlet/en-US/html/TransactionDetails?sid=118ZM.zZYmg9.0&cust_id=368479&link_st... 3/17/2008

111

Stay Details for LARRY SINCLAIR

Property:	Hotel Name	Hotel City
IL142	COMFORT SUITES	GURNEE

Stay Type	Stay Status	CRS Conf #	PMS Conf #	Cancellation #	Reservation Source
Normal	Checked Out	78096854			Source of Stay

Room Type	Payment Method	DOA	LOS	# Rooms	Res. Booked Date	External
SK		11/03/99	3	1		

Hotel Room Rev	Award Eligible Rev	Currency	Exchange Rate	Award Revenue	Total Award
222.00 USD	222.00 USD	1.000000 USD per USD		222.00 USD	2220.00 pts

Expected TAI Date	CRS Hotel TAI Date	SRP Code	Denial	Invoice Property	Trans Date
11/11/99		SCR	N	N	11/21/99

Non-qual Reason			Entry ID

Transaction Details

Promo Code	Description	Award Amount
CCS	US COMFORT HOTELS BASIC STAY	2220.00 pts

http://prodccisapp.chotel.com:8000/cis/servlet/en-US/html/TransactionDetails?sid=118ZM.zZY/mg9.0&cust_id=368479&link_st... 3/17/2008

Page 1 of 1

112

Then let's not forget the statements by Bill Burton and Robert Gibbs,

"Sinclair attempted to extort the Obama campaign for $100,000" and *"Sinclair has been investigated eight times over twenty-five years for blackmail of black politicians,"* both of which were outright lies.

On April 10, 2008, one day after I had appeared via telephone on the number one rated television show in Puerto Rico, SuperXclusivo (detailing Barack Obama's sexual encounters, drug sales and drug use with me in 1999 as well as the fact that Barack Obama was the lover of the murdered Donald Young), Obama attorney Andres W. Lopez told the show's host that, "this person is a mental patient who is a liar, who has engaged in blackmailing of other politicians and was in a mental institution in 1999. He has been a headache to the Obama campaign since last year" (confirming I did indeed contact the campaign in 2007 and asked them to come clean with Obama's 1999 drug use and sales). Mr. Lopez informed the show's host that he was appearing in the capacity of attorney for Barack Obama and Obama for America. In this capacity, Andres W. Lopez went on Puerto Rican television and continued to make outright false statements to attack me. The producer of SuperXclusivo, Maria Acevedo, had contacted me asking me to go on the show. After I appeared on the show, Dailykos.com and the Obama campaign immediately started attacking the television station threatening them and demanding that a spokesperson for Barack Obama be given the opportunity to appear the next day to counter my allegations. The problem with that is, SuperXclusivo intentionally allowed Andres W. Lopez to make false statements, and then refused me the opportunity to rebut Lopez's comments. Maria Acevedo explained to me that the threats, harassment and intimidation directed at the station (in less than twenty-four hours) were more than the owners were willing to deal with. WAPA-TV the broadcasting company of SuperXclusivo was threatened into airing statements by Obama attorney Andres W. Lopez, the station knew to be false and into refusing any rebuttal to Lopez's lies. This is just another example of the many Obama for America attacks made against any media outlet that aired my allegations.

At the same time, all of these attacks were taking place, there were attacks from Obama supporter and board member of the NAACP, Bloomington Commission of the Status of Black Males Commissioner, George W. Tardy, Jr. 2451 E. 10th St. #115, Bloomington, IN 47408-2209 (812) 857-6809 • *Email: mail@gwtardy.com (http://gwtardy.com/)* posting articles implying my demise was imminent with titles like "Rest In Peace Larry Sinclair". In addition to posting "Rest in Peace Larry Sinclair "on the Obama site it was also circulated to ten (10) different pro Obama blogs.

The threats continue to this day, from the three date specific threats to murder me, my mother and my attorney (made via Google's YouTube email system), which on June 16, 2008, the FBI admitted they had located the individual responsible. It ended up that they would not be prosecuting or would they release the identity of the person who made the death threats. Why? Who were the FBI and Assistant U.S. Attorney Patricia Stewart protecting? Shortly after announcing the June 18, 2008 scheduled press conference at the National Press Club in Washington, D.C., I received the following threats:

June 13th, 2008

Oswaldo12345678

  Re: See you at the NPC....

Now you listen to me, faggot. I'm going to kill you, your lawyer and your whore mother. I live in the DC area and you better believe I'm going to gain access to this event. I'm not going to tell you how you will die. It could be an assassin's bullet, vehicle explosion, food poisoning. All you need to know is that your faggot ass is going to die. And, I'm going to get away with it too.

The only way you can save yourself is by calling off this meeting

and ending your smear attacks on Senator Barack Obama.

This and two other similar threats (like this one):

June 15, 2008

Oswaldo12345678

   Re: What happened to Tim Russert could happen to you....
What is the perfect murder? A murder that doesn't get ruled a
murder. Sinclair, there is no amount of security that can protect
you from me. Do you really believe the FBI is going to investigate
your death threats on YouTube? You really are a delusional little
man. Your followers are even more pathetic than you are. I re-
ceived several threats in my PM box shortly after you put my mes-
sage in your blog. One of your followers even claimed to be an
FBI agent. I can only imagine the look on her wrinkled face when
I replied, revealing the fact that I know her full name. I know a lot
more than that. I can gain access to anyone's personal informa-
tion on the internet. Your internet detectives and profilers are
clowns.

I assure you that you should take this threat very seriously. I can kill you any time I want. You could die of a heart attack or a seizure tomorrow and the police would never rule it a murder.

Why am I not afraid to tell you this? Because you claim that your death should be ruled a homicide anyway, and that you get death threats all the time. It doesn't matter what you know, it's what you can prove. You'll never find me and I will get away with killing you. By the way, Chicago is a very nice city. I visited last December. Sinclair, you don't want to end up like Russert, Palfrey and Young. This isn't a game. Don't attend this Press Conference. If you don't die the next day I promise you, you won't live to see the 4th of July.

These were received from an individual that D.C., FBI Special Agent Brenda Borne claimed they identified and told this person not to contact me in any way under any circumstances. This same individual made repeated threats to kill three different people yet the U.S. Attorney for the District of Columbia, Jeffrey Taylor and Assistant U.S. Attorney Patricia Stewart refused to release the identity of this person. Look what this Obama supporter (and I believe employee) wrote immediately after becoming aware that the U.S. Attorney's office was protecting him and his identity:

> *Message from Oswaldo5555555: The threats were a joke?*
>
> *From: YouTube Service (service@youtube.com)*
>
> *Sent: Mon 7/14/08 10:10 a.m.*
>
> *To: larrysinclair0926 (larysinclair0926@hotmail.com)*
>
> *Oswaldo5555555 has sent you a message on YouTube.*
>
> *Re: The threats were a joke.....*

I've been listening to your radio interviews and reading your blog comments, Sinclair. It appears as though my threatening YouTube messages have really upset you. You reported me to the FBI, but you don't appear to be satisfied with the results of their investigation. You've even suggested a conspiracy between U.S. Attorney Jeffrey Taylor and the FBI office to conceal my identity from you, as if you were entitled to it. You've gone as far as to say that you would sue them if they did not provide you with this information. Let me make this clear, I have no intention of killing you or anyone else. The threats were a joke. My motivation was to give you a taste of your own medicine. You are constantly complaining about death threats but are guilty of threatening others, even threatening their families. You know exactly what I am talking about and the FBI is aware of the existence of these threats.

> *The truth is that the FBI did perform a thorough investigation of this case. They traced the email address that was used in the registration of my YouTube account to a specific IP address and internet connection. They went to the residence where this internet connection was installed. I will not confirm or deny whether or not I was identified by the FBI. What I can say, with absolute certainty, is that Special Agent Brenda Born and her partner went to this residence and spoke to an individual who lived there. This individual confessed to writing **my threats** to you but insisted that they had no intentions of acting on them. This individual was interrogated and because they were cooperative, they were not arrested. The residence was not searched, most*

likely, because I did not say how I planned to kill you in the messages. The information from this interrogation was provided to U.S. Attorney Taylor. A background check on the individual who confessed was done. They were not found to have a criminal record of any kind. The threat was not deemed to be credible, therefore no arrest was made and no prosecution is planned.

All of this information could easily be deduced from your own blog comments, including the identity of one of the FBI agents assigned to the case. To prove that my understanding of the case comes from personal knowledge, I will provide the contact information for Special Agent Brenda Born, since you already have it. This information is not available anywhere on the internet so you know that it could only be obtained from some form of contact with this FBI agent:

> *Federal Bureau of Investigation*
> *Brenda K. Born*
> *Special Agent*
> *Washington Field Office*

7799 Leesburg Pike

South Tower Suite 200

Falls Church, VA 22043

Telephone: (202) 278-2000

Fax: (703) 762-3475

Fair enough? I should also inform you that the information you received from a D.C. police officer that you believe describes me is false. I am not, "A 22 year old male living with his parents"

Like I said, I will not confirm or deny that the FBI has identified me. What we both know is that I remain anonymous to you. You do not know my age, gender or living situation. The only information I have given you, about myself, is that I live in the Washington D.C. Metropolitan Area. You do not know my name, address, phone number, email address or any other personal information. You do not know my occupation or who I am associated with. For all you know I work for the FBI or the Obama campaign. For all you know I am not even a single entity. I could

be multiple people who conspired to threaten and intimidate you.

You know me only by my alias, Oswaldo.

At this point, you probably don't know what to believe. You

have been told things about me from multiple sources but nothing

has been verified, similar to your claims about Senator Barack

Obama. The facts are that the FBI investigated your case, I have

no intention of harming you, and you are alive. My advice to you

is to not pursue a lawsuit against the FBI and U.S. Attorney of

D.C. You already have enough legal trouble as it is.

Your lawsuit will be dismissed just like your lawsuit

against Obama, Axelrod and the DNC was. My reason for writing

this message is to clarify that I had no intention of acting on the

previous threats. I am not going to message you again. What you

decide to believe and do at this point is up to you. You can report

this message to Agent Born and try to sue the FBI and U.S. Attor-

ney if they do not have me identified, arrested and prosecuted if you want. You can post this message on your blog, like the others,

to embolden your supporters. That's your decision. I've said all

that I have to say to you. Have a nice life.

Signed,
Oswaldo

Even to this day Assistant U.S. Attorney in Washington, D.C., Patricia Stewart refuses to enforce the law and continues to go out of her way to protect the identity of the person responsible for sending these threats and for mocking her office in the process. The U.S. Attorney for the District of Columbia, Jeffrey Taylor has protected Barack Obama, his employees, supporters and surrogates and has completely ignored the very laws he has sworn to uphold. U.S. Attorney Taylor not only protected an individual from prosecution for death threats, which as a result gave my mother, my attorney and me every reason to be in fear of our lives, but he also was engaged in my false arrest and incarceration on June 18, 2008 in Washington, D.C.

In addition to the constant threats of physical harm, certain arrest, etc., I have been threatened for over a year of being investigated and audited by the Internal Revenue Service. Once Barack Obama was in office, that threat of being investigated by the IRS became reality when I was notified on March 23, 2009, that the Internal Revenue Service had decided to redo my 2008 tax return. When I contacted the IRS concerning them following through on more than a year's threats to investigate me, they responded, "How have you been threatened by the IRS?" Here is just one of the comments about the IRS: "The IRS is going to fuck you harder than your last Mexican boyfriend!"

The Obama administration and surrogates continue to this day to file false complaints with the Internal Revenue Service, Social Security Administration and even the Securities and Exchange Commission for no other purpose than to harass and intimidate me. And, then we have the latest YouTube attempt to harass, threaten and intimidate me by someone using the name "Shadowbloodworth," which I would bet my life is the same person as the "Oswaldo" individual mocking the FBI.

You're a Dead Man

Larry Sinclair;

You are a dead man walking. You're going to rot in prison for your despicable behavior. You're going to die the death of a common criminal. This is the last year you will live on Earth as a free man. That is your destiny. What made you think you could challenge the most powerful man in the world? Do you have any idea what you are up against? You have no idea do you? Let me tell

you. The media blackout, the online smears, the polygraph test

results, the death threats, your arrest, your financial problems

even this very email were all planned by the Obama campaign

and administration. And, you will never be able to prove it. Law

enforcement agencies and attorneys were paid off to oppose or

betray you.

Bloggers were paid to infiltrate your inner circle to spy on

your internet activities. Your personal information, including

your medical records have been accessed and cataloged. Your

computer has been hacked into and every site you visit and email

you make is recorded. Your phones are bugged. People in your

personal life have been paid to report on your everyday conduct.

For every move, you make you will meet a roadblock, and if you

cross the line like you did with your Press Conference last year

you will be arrested again. Had you decided to go to Colorado

during the Democratic National Convention you would be treated

as a security threat and arrested on the spot. You are in grave danger, Larry Sinclair. You are a danger to yourself. You will be dealt with when the time comes. It's all up to Obama when to decide to take action against you. The hope was that if you were ignored long enough you'd just go away. But, you aren't going away are you? You haven't learned your lesson.

Mark my words, Larry Sinclair, you are going to regret having ever spread your filthy lies about President Obama.

This latest attempt was posted on April 23, 2009 which allowed me to insert it in the files prior to printing. FBI Special Agent Brenda Borne was emailed a copy of this latest YouTube threat.

Chapter Ten
The Chicago Police &
Detective Robert McVicker

It was on April 1, 2008 that I submitted a notarized affidavit, via fax, to Chicago Police Department Superintendent Jody Weiss' office concerning my belief that Barack Obama and Trinity United Christian Church Reverend Jeremiah Wright were involved in the murder of Donald Young. This affidavit was forwarded after consulting with my attorney, Montgomery Blair Sibley.

More than three weeks went by after I provided the Chicago police with the affidavit concerning phone conversations I had with a man identifying himself as "Mr. Young" (claiming to be from the Obama Campaign). In fact, the Chicago police ignored the affidavit altogether until the day after Barack Obama was beaten in the Pennsylvania primary by Hillary Clinton by some ten points. When asked why it had taken the Chicago police so long to respond to the affidavit, Homicide Detective Robert McVicker said, "It took a while to filter down from the Superintendent's office to us".

On April 23, 2008 at approximately 9:23 am, I received a

phone call from Detective Robert McVicker asking me to return his call, stating he was calling in regard to the affidavit, I had sent to the Chicago Police Department concerning phone conversations I had with a man claiming to be "Mr. Young" from the Obama Campaign.

Before I had the opportunity to return the call, I received an email from my attorney, Montgomery Blair Sibley, informing me he had spoken with McVicker, and that he was going to call him back and set up a date, so he could meet with me in person. Almost as soon as I posted online that the Chicago police had contacted me regarding the affidavit, Obama supporters and surrogates immediately began contacting the Chicago Police Department making false statements about me in an effort to convince the Chicago police to ignore the sworn affidavit, I provided them.

At first I had thought that McVicker was seriously and honestly investigating the murder of Donald Young. Today I am not so sure. In fact, today I believe the Chicago police only contacted me after the Pennsylvania primary loss suffered by Barack Obama in order to try and help him. Perhaps releasing to the press some statement like, "A Clinton supporter makes false claims against Obama" or something, to that effect. I think what the Chicago police and the Obama campaign did not count on, was my having the phone numbers I had given the Obama camp in the fall of 2007.

There is no doubt in my mind now that the Chicago Police Department was being used by the Obama camp and the office of the Chicago Mayor to attempt to use my affidavit to attack Hillary Clinton. I believe it did not happen, because the Chicago police would have had to engage in the falsification of records and information which would be uncovered by any reasonable investigation.

In my opinion, the Chicago Police Department has let down every citizen in the City of Chicago by failing to investigate completely and accurately the information provided to them in the April 1, 2008 affidavit. Especially since Donald Young himself finally told me who he was, and that he'd gotten my four different phone numbers from Barack Obama personally. It is my belief that the Chicago Police Department has intentionally ignored information in Donald Young's murder for the specific purpose of protecting Barack Obama and Obama's pastor Jeremiah Wright.

It was in early May of 2008, that Det. McVicker notified my attorney that he wanted to talk with me in person the following week. He offered to come to Duluth, Minnesota and meet me at a place and time I determined convenient. I agreed that I would meet with him and informed my attorney. Det. McVicker had stated he wanted to meet that coming Friday or Saturday; I agreed and even changed my schedule to make myself available to him. Just after making sure my schedule was open, I received phone calls from both my attorney and Det. McVicker informing me that Det. McVicker would like to obtain my cell phone records prior to meeting with me in person.

Det. McVicker then asked if I could provide him with all the numbers that Donald Young had contacted me with, and I agreed. I also asked Det. McVicker if he wanted an authorization to release phone records from me, to which he replied, "I will be getting the phone records by way of a grand jury subpoena, which is our normal procedure in these types of things, directly from the cell phone providers".

In May of 2008 in a phone conversation with Det. McVicker, working a rare weekend day, he informed me that his division had been receiving a flood of calls asking to speak with him, yet none of the callers were willing to leave their names or contact numbers when asked. During this same conversation, Det. McVicker stated that he had received a phone call from a man in Texas claiming to be a reporter for the Drudge Report. He was asking questions, to which McVicker replied to the "alleged reporter" that the Chicago police do not comment on open ongoing investigations.

When Det. McVicker told me that a man from Texas had called, I informed the detective that there was a Texas man by the name of Scott Covington. I informed Det. McVicker that Scott Covington was a Houston, Texas piano seller who was under investigation by the Harris County Texas District Attorney's office. He defrauded customers out of more than one million dollars in piano sales that were never delivered to the buyers.

I also informed the detective that this same individual had called and attempted to extort money from my mother, claiming his mother was poor and ill and had sent me her last two hundred dollars for my legal fund, and he wanted that money returned. When he was asked what his mother's name was, he said, "That is not important". When he was asked by my mother what his name was, he again responded, "That is not important".

Well, if he wanted his mother's money returned, her name was extremely important to help find any such contribution, so the money could be returned. However, there never was a two hundred dollar contribution made by his healthy and very wealthy mother who resides in Orange, Texas, with her husband Donald O. Covington (a prominent Republican appointee for Texas Governor Rick Perry). The fact is, Scott Covington called Chicago Police Detective Robert McVicker and provided him false information, claiming to be a representative of the Drudge Report, while, in fact, he was nothing but a demented psychotic Obama internet thug.

Even though Det. McVicker told Covington the Chicago police do not comment on any ongoing investigations, Scott Covington, a convicted felon and black sheep of the family (who cost his father in excess of one million dollars in restitution for fraud) used the internet to claim; "Detective McVicker of the Chicago Police Department stated the phone numbers provided us by Mr. Sinclair show three numbers that have not been in service for more than three years". The problem with the claim made by Scott Covington was that it was a lie.

Scott "Piano Fraud" Covington wrote, "I and others at the Chicago Police Department laugh when they hear the name Larry Sinclair and stated they are tired of that nut case wasting our time…" Covington made no secret of his intentional and dedicated efforts to attack me in trying to protect Barack Obama. His profile on MyBarackObama.com states, "I am from a Republican family and am tired of being told how to vote and who to vote for". What he did not disclose is that he is a convicted felon who defrauded hundreds of individuals out of more than a million dollars selling pianos out of a Houston, Texas business known as The Piano Store at 3701 Kirby Dr. #105, Houston, TX 77098, (713) 524-8449. The Harris County Texas District Attorney's office was diligent enough to hold Covington liable for his fraud.

The only reason Scott Covington is not in a prison cell today is because his father Donald O. Covington, who is legally the president of The Piano Store, repaid more than one million dollars in funds that Scott stole using fraudulent piano sales.

This masquerade by Scott Covington was repeated on a daily basis, multiple times per day, by these internet thugs working for and taking direction from Obama's paid employees David Axelrod; Sam Graham-Felsen; Nate Green; homosexual and adult sex toy artist Eric Gibbons of Fire House Gallery in Bordentown, New Jersey; Ruth Ellen Kessler of Burlington, Massachusetts; and Sheila Bryant, the big mouth bitch from Lawrenceville, Georgia.

All of them not only called the Chicago police repeatedly but also knowingly and intentionally gave false statements by phone to the Chicago Police Department with the sole intent of interfering with their ability to investigate the murder of Donald Young. They all made statements knowing they were untrue just trying to make me look bad.

It was in June of 2008 while in Claymont, Delaware, that I called Chicago Police Detective Robert McVicker to ask if he had obtained my phone records. He said, "Yes, I have received all the records that I had requested through the subpoena". I then explained to Det. McVicker that I was calling to ask if he had obtained them because that very day Sprint/Nextel/Boost informed a paralegal, who was assisting me in obtaining the records, that they do not exist and there is no way to obtain them past the forty-five days they are available online.

Det. McVicker then informed me, "The records are indeed available, but you will have to contact the legal department to obtain them". I then asked Det. McVicker if he would provide a copy of the records to me, and he replied, "I cannot do that because the records are now property of the Chicago Police Department". Through this entire process, Det. McVicker had always treated me with respect and consideration. He made it clear that he understood the swarms of calls to his department were meant to try and prevent him from investigating any of the information provided in my affidavit to the Chicago Police Department. This was a planned and deliberate attempt to interfere with a murder investigation because the Obama surrogates know that Obama was involved with the murder of Donald Young.

As of the writing of this book, Det. McVicker has never contacted me again. I did contact him in October, November and December 2008 to inquire as to whether the Chicago police had made any arrests in the Donald Young murder. Det. McVicker stated, "We have not made any arrest nor do we have any suspect at this time."

Since first contacting the Chicago Police Department and then sending them the affidavit on April 1, 2008, the Obama for America campaign, as well as the Obama bloggers have engaged in acts of intimidation and threats. I believe these tactics have resulted in the Chicago Police Department intentionally failing to investigate legitimate leads in the murder of Donald Young. By that, the Chicago Police Department has done a disservice to the family of Donald Young and the citizens of Chicago.

Chapter Eleven
The Clinton Connection

After going public with the YouTube video on January 17, 2008, I was buried in emails and phone calls from all over. People wanted me to contact the Hillary Clinton Campaign. I repeatedly explained to these people that I had no intention of contacting the campaign of any candidate with my allegations against Barack Obama. It was hard to explain to these people that I did not go public with the information about Barack Obama to help another candidate, but in fact, that is exactly what the media and Barack Obama's own campaign staff were claiming. I intended on remaining apolitical in respect to the campaign. My only desire was for Barack Obama to be honest with the American people and admit the fact that he was using and selling cocaine in November 1999 while serving as an Illinois State Senator, and that he did engage in homosexual activity with me. After experiencing the unrelenting attacks by the Obama campaign and its supporters for months, I decided to go to Washington, D.C. in May 2008 for the Democratic National Committee's Rules and By-Laws Committee meeting. I had filed repeated complaints with the DNC earlier and decided to confront them in person for their refusal to acknowledge the complaints filed with them.

In the months prior to May 2008 I had contacted several respected Democrats concerning the facts about Barack Obama. In February 2008 I contacted former Vice President Walter Mondale's law offices in an effort to retain the former Vice President as legal counsel. I spoke with Vice President Mondale's executive secretary that assured me she would speak with the Vice President when he returned to town and get back with me. It was just a few days later that the Vice President's secretary contacted me and informed me that Vice President Mondale could not represent me. It was a short time later, after Senator John Edwards had withdrawn from the Democratic Presidential Primary, that I contacted his Chapel Hill, North Carolina offices.

When I called John Edwards' Chapel Hill, North Carolina campaign office, a man answered the phone. I had asked the man if this was John Edwards' office, and if he spoke with Senator Edwards personally. The man stated he did speak with Senator Edwards personally on a daily basis. I then informed the man that my name was Larry Sinclair, and that I have made truthful and factual allegations against Barack Obama; that I believe Senator Edwards needs to be aware of them before he publicly endorses any candidate. The man asked what the allegations were. I then explained to Senator Edwards' representative how I had met Barack Obama in November 1999, and how he (Obama) had purchased/sold an eight ball of cocaine for/to me and how Barack Obama, and I had engaged in a sexual act in the back of a limo that I had rented. I informed the representative of Senator Edwards how Barack Obama had pulled out a glass crack pipe while I was performing oral sex on him and how Obama had smoked at least two crack cocaine rocks while receiving a blow job from me. I then explained how the following day Barack Obama had arrived at my Gurnee, Illinois hotel room unannounced and uninvited, offering me even more cocaine while asking for a second blow job and smoking more crack cocaine.

After explaining everything to Senator Edwards' representative I was told that Senator Edwards would be given the message as well as my name and phone number. After not hearing back from Senator Edwards' office, I contacted Senator Edwards' former law firm. I asked that they get a message to Senator Edwards to please contact Larry Sinclair and gave them my phone numbers for Senator Edwards to reach me.

At the same time, I was contacting Senator John Edwards in Chapel Hill, North Carolina, I was advised in an anonymous phone call to contact attorney Lanny Davis. I 'Googled' Lanny Davis' name, and while I found he had connections to the Clintons, nothing said he was on the staff of the Hillary Clinton Campaign. I sent Mr. Davis an email explaining who I was, and what

I had publicly stated about Barack Obama. While I did not speak directly with Lanny Davis concerning my allegations against Barack Obama, I began receiving phone calls from people who stated they were contacting me at the request of Mr. Davis. The individuals were contacting me but wanted to give me advice without me knowing to whom I was talking. I had a real problem with that.

In some of these phone conversations I was being told that Howard Wolfson and Mark Penn had been informed of my allegations against Barack Obama, and they were relaying advice directly from Howard Wolfson and Mark Penn. I had a problem with this because I did not want anyone to try and say I was making claims against Obama to help Hillary Clinton. For those readers who do not know who Howard Wolfson and Mark Penn are, both were Hillary Clinton Campaign managers. I was starting to feel very uncomfortable with the calls from people who would not identify themselves and whose phone numbers could not be identified. It was only after going to Washington, D.C. for the May 31, 2008 Democratic National Committee Rules and By-Laws Committee meeting at the Marriott Wardman Park Hotel that people started contacting me and giving me their names. Upon my arrival at the Marriott, I noticed a man wearing Democratic National Committee credentials talking to hotel security and pointing at me. Shortly after observing this exchange between hotel security and the DNC official, I was approached by hotel security and told, "Sir, you cannot have that sign here." When I asked, "Why?" security replied, "No signs are allowed." It was at this time I pointed out the signs being carried by everyone both inside and outside of the hotel. Security then stated, "That sign cannot be on hotel property; either you leave the property, or you will be arrested." It was at this time that I advised hotel security I would register as a Marriott guest, and he responded, "You still cannot have that sign on hotel property." The sign simply announced that Barack Obama was a liar and that Donald Young was murdered to protect Barack Obama. I went to the DNC representative and told him I would see to it that his face was plastered all over the internet and that these events would be documented.

During the time I spent at the Rules and By-Laws Committee meeting in Washington, D.C. on May 31, 2008 many individuals approached me. One individual who approached me was a lady that I will identify as "Dale." Dale claimed that she was a private investigator and stated, "Larry, I will do anything I can to help you, but you have to give me everything you have. You have to give me the limo driver's name, the name of the person whose graduation you attended; everything." Well, I had learned my lesson from offers like this made in months prior to my trip to D.C., so I took the woman's phone number and did speak with her a couple of times, but I did not feel she was for real. In fact, to this day, I still have no last name for her or any name for the investigation firm. There is just the name "Dale" and the phone number 415-203-8430.

It was "Dale" who had called a friend of hers who was inside the Marriott Wardman Park Hotel for the Democratic National Committee's Rules and By-Laws Committee meeting. She asked him to locate me and tell me to leave the meeting and get over to a Clinton rally at a park a couple of blocks from the Marriott. While sitting in the Starbuck's at the Marriott, a man came up to me and passed me a cell phone. The lady "Dale" said, "Larry get over to the park, Greta is here and wants to meet you." I then asked for directions to the Clinton rally and found "Dale" standing next to Greta Van Susteren. It was through "Dale" that (as I had reported after the Obama campaign began trying to smear Greta) I introduced myself to Greta Van Susteren and I told her, "Greta, if you want to talk, I will answer ANY questions you ask and give you any information you request." I then shook Greta's hand and at Greta's request provided her a phone number where I could be reached. On the walk from the park back to the Marriott, I was accompanied by Eve Fairbanks of New

Republic.com.

After returning to the Marriott Wardman Park, I decided to return to my hotel, as I was in severe pain from the walking, standing and sitting. I had not made it a mile away from the Marriott before my cell phones started ringing off the hook. I received a call from a lady (because I respect her dearly, and have become good friends with her) I will only refer to as "Auntie M." I met with Auntie M and Stephanie at their request at the Omni Hotel around nine thirty in the evening May 31, 2008. During the meeting, we discussed my allegations about Barack Obama; the attacks and efforts to shut me up that came after my posting of the original YouTube video. While Auntie M and Stephanie were Hillary Clinton supporters; they were not "employees" of the Clinton Campaign nor were they fund raisers. It turns out that Auntie M and Stephanie were being used as contact middlemen for a very wealthy Clinton supporter who wanted to help get the truth out. After our discussion and answering questions we said, "Goodnight," and I returned to my hotel.

It was the very next day Sunday, June 1, 2008 that I began receiving calls from Dale the private investigator, asking me even more questions. It was during one of these calls that she asked if I had been contacted by "BFF." Note: BFF is an individual who began contacting me shortly after I appeared at the Democratic

National Committees Rules and By-Laws Committee meeting the night before. The calls from "BFF" were coming from 415-407-9978. I had several voice mails from both Dale and "BFF" telling me that they wanted me to meet with a gentleman named "Eric" and that he had been given my phone number and would be calling me to set up a meeting. I had no idea who this "Eric" was other than I was told he was a good friend of "BFF's." I was told that "Eric" would contact me before the end of the day. I was also told that "Eric" would help me get the truth out about Barack Obama, and that I could trust him with everything.

It was Monday and I still had not heard from "Eric." I continued getting calls and voice messages from "Dale" asking if I had spoken with "Eric" yet. After about five or six calls and voice messages asking if I had spoken to "Eric," I called "BFF" and asked who they were and who this "Eric" was that I was supposed to talk with. Well "BFF" turned out to be a lady by the name of Susie Tompkins Buell. I had no idea who Susie Buell was. The following was obtained from the Susie Tompkins Buell Foundation web site:

Susie Tompkins Buell was the founder and co-owner of the Esprit clothing company, which was known for its revolutionary fusion of corporate mission with social responsibility. The Esprit Foundation was created in 1990 and supported a variety of organizations in areas such as at-risk youth, AIDS awareness and direct care, women's issues and the environment.

When Susie Tompkins Buell left Esprit de Corp in 1996, she took the Foundation with her and eventually renamed it the Susie Tompkins Buell Foundation. The Foundation retained the original mission and areas of funding, including a "women and girls lens," which screened organizations for their inclusion of women and girls, not only as recipient of services but also for their representation on boards and staff.

Today the Susie Tompkins Buell Foundation carries on the original spirit of innovation and social responsibility in its grant making interests and practices.

This was obtained from Wikipedia:

Susie Tompkins Buell is an American entrepreneur and a liberal political donor associated with the Democracy Alliance. Buell has been described in a podcast as "one of the most successful women entrepreneurs of all time."

In 1967, Tompkins Buell and Jane Tise co-founded the Plain Jane clothing label. Plain Jane was making two million dollars a year by 1970. Tompkins Buell's new husband Douglas Tompkins recommended changing the name to Esprit. Clashes with the ex-

isting partners of Esprit led to a buyout in 1975. By 1986, the global clothing brand had reached eight hundred million dollars in sales. The Tompkins' divorced in 1988.

The early sensibility of Esprit was seen as flowing from the personalities and interests of its founders. They were once described as "a pair of San Francisco hippie merchants who sold clothing over a North Beach massage parlor."

After the 1988 divorce, Tompkins Buell led a 1990 leveraged buyout that allowed her to gain control of Esprit, and also earned her a profit of about one hundred fifty (150) million dollars. The buyout left Esprit deeply in debt. In two years, it went into technical default on its outstanding loans and in 1997 Tompkins Buell relinquished all ownership of and involvement in the company to a consortium of investors.

In March 1997, Tompkins Buell sued the new owners of Esprit for $3 million, she said they owed her in reimbursement for tax payments. Her ex-husband declined to file a similar lawsuit, saying he thought the legal basis for such a suit was thin. In response to the lawsuit, Jay Margolis, the new CEO of Esprit, barred Buell and all members of her family from entering Esprit headquarters.

Buell is often described as Hillary Clinton's best friend.

Buell led Clinton's fundraising efforts for 2008 in the San Francisco Bay area. In 2006, the Washington Post published a story about the Democracy Alliance, calling it an "exclusive donor club" for progressive donors and identifying Buell and her husband Mark Buell as members.

Buell held a fundraiser for David Brock's "Media Matters" at her San Francisco home. A foundation that bears her name gave money to Media Matters through the Tides Foundation.

When I first spoke with "Susie" I had no idea how close she was to Hillary Clinton. It was in the first conversation with Susie that I was told who "Eric" was. She said his name was Eric Mullen, that he was connected in D.C., and that I could trust him with everything. Susie then asked me to trust Eric and to work with him and give him whatever he asked for. Then she gave me his cell phone number and asked me to call him if I did not hear from him by the end of the day. Shortly after the call to Susie I received a call from Eric Mullen. Again, I had no idea who Eric Mullen was or what kind of work he did. It was only after my arrest and incarceration at the National Press Club in Washington, D.C. on June 18, 2008 that I had become aware of exactly who Eric Mullen was and why Susie said he was connected in D.C. Not only was Eric Mullen close to Bill and Hillary Clinton and Lanny Davis, but his wife, Kelly Craighead was Hillary or Bill

Clinton's chief assistant in the Clinton White House. Susie, Eric and Dale disclosed none of this when all these people were asking me to work with them. I had asked each of them if they were involved in the Hillary Clinton Campaign and each of them responded that they were not. I find out later that was not the case and that this was not just your average Hillary supporter. In September and October 2008 while speaking with Susie Buell and her friends I am told how Susie is just devastated because she is being pressured to support Obama and raise money for him, and she just does not want to do it. However, according to political contribution records, Susie Buell donated three thousand one hundred (3,100) dollars on September 17, 2008 to the Obama Victory Fund and another one thousand (1,000) dollars on October 14, 2008, just days after I left her a voice message asking a friend of hers to relay her message to me.

The first call from Eric Mullen was to ask if we could meet in person for lunch and I agreed. Due to Eric caring for a newborn, that meeting was canceled and rescheduled. It was then that Eric Mullen had contacted me and asked if I would be willing to meet with a friend of his, a reporter from Bloomberg News (who at this time I have decided not to identify due to a story this reporter is still working on). I agreed. My first meeting took place at Fourteen K, the restaurant at the Hamilton Plaza Hotel in

Washington, D.C. with the reporter from Bloomberg News. The first part of our meeting was spent checking the reporter's identification and providing mine. Then we moved into my providing him with copies of documents, including my medical records, copies of the original Colorado warrant, credit card statements from 1999, names and phones numbers etc.... It was at this time, I began answering questions as well as getting some information confirming that my 1999 limo driver, Jagir Multani, was known to have been engaged in a lucrative business arrangement with Obama fundraiser and friend, Tony Rezko. In addition to confirming the relationship between Multani and Rezko, I was also told it was known why Multani had become difficult to find, but I was never told the reason.

The day the verdict found Tony Rezko guilty in Chicago, I was asked to meet the Bloomberg News reporter on the rooftop of his office building. Needless to say just the thought of meeting someone in Washington, D.C. on a rooftop was enough to make anyone uneasy. After several meetings between the Bloomberg News reporter and me, Eric Mullen finally appeared for one of the meetings. I immediately asked Eric, "I hope you are not offended, but would you happen to have some ID on you?" Mullen, an easy-going man with thinning hair handed me his driver's license and then began by asking me, "Would you be willing to take another polygraph if Bloomberg set it up?" I immediately replied, "Yes." Mullen then asked, "Would you be willing to sign release authorization forms for Bloomberg, allowing them to obtain your cell phone records and for Citibank allowing them to obtain your credit card statements?" Again my reply was immediate without even the slightest hesitation, "Yes." After meeting for almost four hours on this windy, rainy, June afternoon in D.C. at Fourteen K, we decided to end it there for now. Before leaving, Eric Mullen looked at me and said, "You do not need to take another polygraph, the fact that you agreed to it without hesitation is enough for me." Just before ending the meeting, Eric explained to me what he thought needed to be done. Eric had begun to explain that the Obama people had done an excellent job in making me look like a fruitcake with all the sparring on the internet. Eric said that his plan was to take the information and begin to build bridges. He explained, "You are on an island, and what we need to do is build bridges between you and the mainland. With each piece of information, we need to connect; each connection becomes a bridge." As Eric Mullen gets up to leave, he pauses, looks at me for a few seconds and then says, "I want you to go home to Duluth, go back to living your life, ignore everything being written about you on the internet, stop blogging and let us handle this." When Eric Mullen made those statements to me, I started to have reservations as to exactly what it was that

150

Susie Buell, Eric Mullen, Dale (the alleged California private investigator), Auntie M and Stephanie were really wanting. After a total of nine days in Washington, D.C. meeting with various people who contacted me; after hearing Eric Mullen say he had Donald Young's phone numbers in his cell phone, and telling me he believed me; while at the same time he was telling me to go home and act like nothing happened; I went back to Duluth, Minnesota more confused than ever.

Before leaving Washington, I contacted Democratic National Committee co-chair Donna Brazile and asked for a personal face-to-face meeting with her. At first, Ms. Brazile tried to act as if she had no idea who I was. I learned then Ms. Brazile really knew how to play the "stupid" role to a "T." After an extensive email exchange with Donna Brazile confronting her for referring to me as a liar and a racist, she sent me an email from her beloved "Blackberry" asking me not to publish her emails on the blog. Needless to say Donna Brazile would not agree to a face-to-face meeting, but her emails made it clear that she was going to continue to work in the background to attack me and assist in the attacks any way she could. I guess for Donna Brazile "Cooking with grease" made her head like lard.

After a final meeting with the Bloomberg News reporter and Eric Mullen, I returned to Duluth, Minnesota. After nine in-

151

teresting days in Washington, I was glad to be home, even if it would only be for a short while before returning to D.C. and The National Press Club. Between my return home and my National Press Club appearance, the phone did not stop buzzing the entire time. There were text messages from Eric Mullen, 202-409-8803; voice messages from the Bloomberg News reporter; calls from Auntie M and Susie Buell, 415-407-9978; Dale, 415-203-8430; and messages from other people too. Who they were, I had no idea.

Chapter Twelve
D.C. Arrest & the Biden Connection

Anti-Obama Blogger Faces No Felony Charge

Friday, September 5, 2008

Delaware News Journal Page B3

Staff Report

Charges against a Barack Obama critic, who was arrested for allegedly using counterfeit money orders to pay for a three-week stay at a New Castle hotel in 2007, were dropped last week.

Larry Sinclair's Newark attorney, Fran E. Farren, said he and his client were happy that prosecutors dismissed the felony charge against Sinclair.

"All along, it was our position that this case was more 'civil' than 'criminal' and that Mr. Sinclair was guilty of no criminal act," Farren said.

"Mr. Sinclair has asserted his innocence since he was initially arrested and we are quite pleased that we were able to con-

vince the state to dismiss the charge against him. It was the proper thing to do."

Sinclair, of Duluth, Minn., has made charges about Obama involving sex and drugs on his blog.

Sinclair was arrested in June on an outstanding warrant after a Washington, D.C., news conference.

According to Delaware State Police and Delaware Superior Court records, Sinclair paid for a three week stay at a Rodeway Inn with $2,400 in money orders.

The hotel manager later told police Wachovia refused to honor them.

The editor of the Wilmington, Delaware paper The News Journal repeatedly published outright lies about my arrest and the alleged charges against me. They continued to repeat the same blatantly false information even after the charges had been dismissed on August 28, 2008.

It was June 2008 when Joe and Beau Biden, the father and son team from Delaware, began to institute the final phase of their plan to gain favor with the Democratic primary front runner Barack Obama. This plan began in January 2008 and on January

3, 2008 Delaware Senator Joe Biden announced that he was drop-
ping out of the race to become the Democratic nominee for President of the United States. On January 17, 2008 I posted my original YouTube video, in which I accused Barack Obama of lying
about his drug use. I also went public about Barack Obama's
closet homosexual relationships and sexual encounters.

On February 4, 2008 (a couple of weeks after going public
about Obama's sell and use of cocaine and gay sex encounters)
Joseph (Beau) R. Biden III, Delaware Attorney General, through
Susan Dwyer, Deputy Attorney General brought a sealed Grand
Jury indictment against me.

IN THE SUPERIOR COURT OF THE STATE OF DELAWARE

IN AND FOR NEW CASTLE COUNTY

STATE OF DELAWARE	)	
	)	
V.	)	INDICTMENT BY THE GRAND JURY
	)	I.D.# 0712005646
LAWRENCE W. SINCLAIR	)	IN _____ 08 - 02 - 0080u

The Grand Jury charges **LAWRENCE W. SINCLAIR** with the following offense, a Felony;

THEFT, in violation of Title 11, Section 841 of the Delaware Code of 1974, as amended.

LAWRENCE W. SINCLAIR, on or about the 16th day of October, 2007, in the County of New Castle, State of Delaware, did take, exercise control over, or obtain property of Rodeway Inn or another person, consisting of United States Currency or other miscellaneous property valued at $1,000.00 or more, intending to deprive that person and/or the owner of same, or to appropriate same.

A TRUE BILL

(signature)
(FOREPERSON)

JOSEPH R. BIDEN, III
ATTORNEY GENERAL

(signature)
DEPUTY ATTORNEY GENERAL

156

The Foreperson on the Grand Jury was involved in the Delaware Campaign of Barack Obama. We will return to this later.

I arrived in Washington, D.C. on the evening of June 14, 2008 for a scheduled press conference at the National Press Club on June 18, 2008. My arrival was earlier than I had originally planned due to receiving several threats to kill me, my mother and my attorney, Montgomery Blair Sibley if I did not cancel my press conference. My arrival date and time as well as where I would be staying while in D.C. was provided to both the FBI and the D.C. Metro Police. They had been investigating the death threats I received a week before my press conference. Now this is very important that you remember, because you are going to see very clearly how my eventual arrest on June 18, 2008 was carefully planned and choreographed for maximum impact in the Obama campaign's attempt to discredit me. You are also going to see how the FBI, D.C. Metro Police and the President and General Manager of the National Press Club were all involved. It was Beau and Joe Biden's effort to earn political favor and eventually the position of Vice President and to Biden's son the future "gift" of Delaware's U.S. Senatorial seat. The Delaware News Journal decided not to report any of this because they were too busy spending the summer of 2008 publishing articles about me that

157

they *KNEW* were false. All of this lying and conniving was in an (successful) effort to protect Joe Biden, Beau Biden and Barack Obama.

It was June 18, 2008, and I had just finished my press conference in the Holeman Lounge at the National Press Club. In the days leading up to the press conference the blog Fire Dog Lake and MSNBC's loud mouth piece of sh*t, Keith Olbermann went on a full frontal assault against me and the National Press Club. Fire Dog Lake bloggers showed up at the National Press Club to deliver signatures they claim to have collected on the internet demanding that the National Press Club cancel their press conference contract with me. It was not until after all had been said and done, that the words of the NPC Manager to the Obama worshiping idiots from Fire Dog Lake became clear. The National Press Club wanted to keep the money they had charged me to rent the room, while at the same time helping the Obama and Biden idiots organize my arrest!

Prior to my arrival in Washington, I had provided the D.C. office of the FBI and the Metro Police the following information on June 13, 2008. My flight itinerary: US Airways Flight Number 1028 departing Minneapolis/St Paul June 14, 2008 at 5:20 PM arriving Charlotte, North Carolina at 8:53 PM; US Airways Flight Number 302 departing Charlotte, North Carolina at 10:00 PM

June 14, 2008 arriving Washington, D.C. National Airport June 14, 2008 at 11:22 PM. Upon arriving in Washington, I was picked up at Reagan National Airport by the same driver that was hired to drive me during my May 31, 2008 Washington trip. When I arrived at my hotel, I contacted both the D.C. Metro Police and the Washington FBI office and provided them with the name and phone number of my hotel as well as my room number. Keep in mind that during the entire time leading up to the June 18, 2008 National Press Club news conference, the D.C. Police and FBI knew exactly where I was and yet no arrest took place. The alleged "fugitive from justice" warrant that was served me after my press conference, has to this day never been produced by the D.C. Police, the U.S. Attorney for the District of Columbia or anyone else. However, we will get back to that shortly.

After arriving at my hotel I learned that my luggage containing the press passes for the news conference along with other material was lost. On Sunday morning, June 15, 2008 while on my way to the airport to check on my luggage I was contacted by Northwest airlines in Newark, New Jersey. They informed me my luggage was at their airport and was being re-routed back to Washington's National airport on a Continental flight to arrive at 12:20 PM. The luggage never showed up and was later found to be at the Charles de Gaulle International Airport in Paris, France.

Because of this, I spent all of Monday, June 16, 2008 having new press passes made and delivered. I also had to re-do the press statement (which contained the usual Montgomery Blair Sibley typos that I could not correct before the press conference and had to instruct the press to correct during the press conference), in addition to having to purchase all new clothing for the press conference. All of this happening while being told by a D.C. FBI Special Agent on Monday, June 16, 2008 that she had spoken with the individual who had threatened to murder me at the press conference. However, she was instructed by the U.S. Attorney of the District of Columbia that she could not provide me or my attorney with the name of this individual. Special Agent Borne informed me that the person threatening my life would not contact me and would not be anywhere near the National Press Club building on June 18, 2008. When asked if the Washington, D.C. Police had been informed, Special Agent Borne replied that the D.C. Metro Police was also involved in the questioning of the person known to me and my attorney only as "Oswaldo...."

Because of the security issue (due to the threats to gain access to the NPC event to "kill" people), my attorney and I met with the National Press Club staff on Monday June 16, 2008 around 1:30 in the afternoon to go over security arrangements. A couple of hours after meeting with George Arfken of the NPC, and going over how my attorney and I would conduct the press conference, I received a phone call back from Mr. Arfken. He informed me that he had just gotten out of a meeting with the General Manager and the National Press Club building's director of security. The three of them had set out a plan for my arrival, entrance, and exit into and out of the National Press Club.

George Arfken emailed me the plan after informing me of it by phone. The General Manager Bill McCarren, Assistant G M David King, and George Arfken decided I was to arrive at 12:45 PM. I was to enter the building from the F Street side and go up one floor to a key controlled glass elevator. I would be met there by the NPC Director of Security and escorted up to the 13th floor. Once I arrived, I was to wait in a closed bar area next to the Holeman Lounge while my attorney and the security guard I hired handled the press sign up. In the meantime, the NPC was setting up the broadcast camera and equipment for filming the press conference. The National Press Club insisted that I remain in the bar area next to the Holeman Lounge until the press conference was ready to begin. When the press conference was over (per the instructions of NPC GM Bill McCarren and Assistant GM David King), I was to return to the bar next to the Holeman Lounge and wait there until everyone had been cleared out of the *Holeman* Lounge. I would then be escorted out of the National Press Club through the back key controlled elevator that I had entered from. The complaint by the press that my Attorney Montgomery Blair Sibley denied the media access to me at the end of the press conference was, in fact, the decision and instructions of managers Bill McCarren and David King. The same National Press Club General Managers that made the following statement to representatives of Fire Dog Lake on June 16, 2008. *"Hopefully this man will be exposed for what he really is."*

Before the beginning of the press conference Assistant GM David King asked Mr. Sibley and I to make a statement. The statement was as follows: "The National Press Club is not a sponsor of this event and is not involved in any manner other than the normal act of renting its facilities." Both Sibley and I made that very clear. In addition to the request for that statement, I was informed after the press conference that the National Press Club had intentionally omitted placing the NPC logo on the podium and on the wall behind the podium. However, the NPC had no problem collecting the full charges for these services. ($4,840.70).

Despite all the efforts by MSNBC's Keith Olbermann, Fire Dog Lake, Daily Kos, Huffington Post, etc., the press conference did indeed take place as scheduled.

The following is the statement I read at the press conference on June 18, 2009. The typos in the original written statement prepared by Montgomery Blair Sibley have been corrected.

PRESS STATEMENT OF LARRY SINCLAIR JUNE 18, 2008

Good afternoon. My name is Larry Sinclair, and I am a former recreational drug user and trafficker, a convicted felon for crimes of forgery, bad checks and theft by check. I am also an American who loves this country, and I cannot stay silent regarding Barack Obama, knowing what I know.

Today I will discharge my obligation as a citizen to witness this knowledge to you and raise questions for others to investigate and consider. I am going to briefly describe my background, my experience with Senator Obama in 1999, what appears to me to be a coordinated effort to discredit me and finally a list of questions. After this brief statement, I will take and try to answer any reasonable questions.

Background

I am 46 years old, and I currently reside in Duluth, MN. I am a U.S.Citizen, and I have made mistakes in my lifetime. I have been convicted and served prison sentences for writing bad

163

checks, forging checks, using stolen credit card numbers in Arizona, Florida and Colorado. These events occurred over twenty (20) years ago between 1980 through 1986.

After going public on the internet with these claims against Senator Obama earlier this year, I became aware of a warrant out of Florida from 1986 which I have resolved, and it has now been dismissed. I also have an active "Colorado Only" warrant for alleged "Theft and Forgery". I am not ignoring this warrant but am addressing it with the Court in Colorado as well as with the DA's office. I have a pending motion to dismiss this warrant which I am waiting to have calendared by the Colorado Court.

I have lived and worked under three different names. My birth name is Lawrence W. Sinclair. Later, I had my name legally changed first to La-Rye A. Silvas, and then La-Rye Vizcarra Avila. The last two were legal name changes granted by the court in Penal County Superior Court, Florence, Arizona. I legally returned to my birth name in the Fremont County District Court, Canon City, Colorado in 1997.

Obama Incident

I flew out of Colorado Springs, Colorado to Chicago on November 2, 1999, arriving at O'Hare early in the morning of

November 3, 1999. I traveled to the Chicago area to attend the graduation of my Godson (my best friend's son) from basic training at the Great Lakes Navy Training Center. I made reservations at the Comfort Inn and Suites in Gurnee, IL based on the location to the Navy Training Center.

On November 5, 1999, I hired the services of Five Star Limo. I hired them for both November 5ᵗʰ and 6ᵗʰ. On November 6ᵗʰ, I asked the limo driver (whose name I now reveal for the first time) Jagir Multani, if he knew anyone who would like to socialize and show me Chicago. Mr. Multani understood that I was looking for someone who knew Chicago and would enjoy socializing. He said he knew someone who was a friend of his.

On November 6, 1999 after picking me up at my hotel in Gurnee (and this is significant), Jagir Multani used his cell phone to make a call. That call was made to then Illinois State Senator Barack Obama. He proceeded to set up an introduction between me and Senator Obama. Upon arriving at the bar and exiting the limo, Senator Obama was standing next to Jagir Multani as I was introduced to Senator Obama. Later that evening at a bar which I believe was called Alibis; I mention I could use a line or two to wake up. Senator Obama asked me if I was referring to "coke" and after stating I was, he stated that he could purchase cocaine for me. He then made a telephone call (and this too, is signifi-

165

cant) from his cell phone to an unknown individual during which Senator Obama arranged the cocaine purchase.

Senator Obama and I then departed from the bar in my limousine and proceeded to an unknown location. Obama exited the limousine with two hundred fifty dollars ($250), I had given him and returned shortly with an "eight-ball" of cocaine. I ingested a couple of lines of cocaine, and shortly thereafter Senator Obama produced a glass cylinder pipe and packet of crack cocaine from his pants pocket. Obama proceeded to smoke the crack cocaine. I performed fellatio on Senator Obama in the limousine during the time he was smoking crack cocaine; afterwards I had the driver take me to my hotel (The Comfort Inn, Gurnee, Illinois).

The following day, November 7, 1999, Senator Obama appeared at my hotel room where we again ingested cocaine, and I again performed fellatio on him.

Significantly, both the driver's telephone call to Senator Obama and his call to the drug dealer should appear on the driver's and Senator Obama's cell phone billing statements.

Fall 2007

In September 2007 I contacted the Presidential Campaign of Barack H. Obama, to request solely that Senator Obama pub-

166

licly correct his stated drug use record to reflect his use of crack cocaine with me in November 1999. When I made that first contact I left the Presidential Campaign of Senator Barack H. Obama a telephone number for them to return my call. The first number I provided was a Texas cell phone number.

From the period of Labor Day weekend 2007 through November 18, 2007 I provided a total of four (4) different callback numbers to the Obama campaign, as I had moved and had changed the numbers to reflect locally my place of residence at the time. In late September to early October 2007, I received a call from a male who identified himself as a "Mr. Young" stating he was calling in regard to calls, I had made to the Obama campaign. This first call was, in fact, an attempt by "Mr. Young" to obtain from me the identities of anyone I might have contacted concerning my 1999 allegations against Senator Obama. This first call shocked me in that this "Mr. Young" asked me why I had not asked Senator Obama to disclose the sexual encounters we had in 1999. I was shocked because I had never mentioned to the campaign or anyone working for the campaign any sexual encounters as my call was prompted by drug allegations only. The call ended with "Mr. Young" stating I would hear from someone in a few days.

In mid to late October 2007, I received a second call from this "Mr. Young" at which time I clearly became aware that this individual was personally involved with Senator Obama rather than just an employee of his campaign. The tone of the conversation had a sexual nature. "Mr. Young" did not once advise me how he obtained my phone number which by this time had now changed to a Delaware number.

In late October 2007, I received a text message from the gentleman identified as "Mr. Young" in which he stated he was intimately involved with Senator Obama and that Obama was discussing with him and his pastor how to publicly acknowledge Obama's drug use in 1999. Obama wanted to be sure I had not discussed the sexual encounters or drug incidents with any media at that time.

In mid to late November 2007, in another text message from "Mr. Young" , he advised me that Senator Obama will publicly correct his statement as to the last time he used drugs, and I need not concern myself with publicly disclosing it.

The last contact I had with "Mr. Young" was in early December 2007 when he made it clear to me that Senator Obama had no intentions of publicly acknowledging his 1999 use of crack cocaine. He also said that he was, in fact, doing nothing more than milking information from me for Senator Obama's use.

I later learned that a Donald Young was the choir director of Reverend Wright's Trinity United Church of Christ (Obama's former church), and was openly a homosexual. I also learned that he was murdered on December 23, 2007.

I have cooperated with the Chicago Police Department in this matter by providing them the telephone numbers I was using during the fall of 2007. I will release them now publicly in the hopes that someone may be able to connect the dots between these telephone numbers and Mr. Young. Those numbers are: 956-758-1105; 956-758-1885; 956-758-8002; 302-685-7175; 612 -466-1043.

In what I now realize was a naive and un-counseled decision, in January 2008, I posted a video on YouTube.com where I related the above information regarding my liaisons with Senator Obama in 1999. The response was overwhelming and I quickly became the recipient of what in hindsight appears to have been a coordinated attack on my character with ever increasing falsehoods circulating on the internet. In response I agreed to take a polygraph test from Whitehouse.com. The results of that test had been partially revealed, which resulted in labeling me a liar and taken as gospel by all.

I would like to make the following comments about that

polygraph test. First, I have been subsequently advised that Whitehouse.com was a website dedicated to anti-Clinton pornography until earlier this year. Second, I have now come to understand that lie detectors are junk science at best, which is why courts of law refuse to use them. Third, a review of the results by George W. Maschke, Ph.D. of AntiPolygraph.org raises serious questions about the legitimacy of the examination. Indeed, overlooked by almost everyone is that Whitehouse.com's own examiner, Dr. Gordon Barland, observed that on the drug question regarding Senator Obama, the computerized score found that there was less than a 1% probability of deception by me. That's about as high a passing score as one can possibly attain.

Finally, in February 2008 I was told anonymously that Dan Parisi of Whitehouse.com received $750,000 from the Obama campaign through AKR Media to organize an effort to publicly discredit me. When I confronted Parisi with this allegation, he did not deny it but instead withdrew the second exonerating polygraph report of Dr. Gordon Barland. He also failed to post the video of my polygraph as he and Whitehouse.com promised they would do. He even removed posts from their web site altogether, claiming that they had "had enough of the attacks by Sinclair's supporters and Sinclair himself."

The polygraph results (though misrepresented) were im-

mediately seized upon by the blogger community, and I became the subject of vicious lies about me. I was forced to file a lawsuit in an attempt to stop those lies about me that have been circulating. That lawsuit sought to obtain the proof of what I was saying about my contact with Senator Obama. I was doing this through subpoenas for the identities of the anonymous bloggers, so they could be linked to the Obama campaign and relevant records of the cell phone companies to prove the truth of my allegations. To date, though the lawsuit is now over ninety days old, Judge Kennedy has refused to permit the suit to move forward so this evidence may be obtained.

Conclusion

In summation, you can discredit my story and then make your decision on who should be the next President of the United States. The burden is now off of me as I have told my story without the distortions. These distortions have been intentionally heaped on me in what my lawyer calls an ad hominem attack – shoot the messenger so you don't have to hear the message he is bringing. I am now done. It is for others to find the corroborating evidence of my story by locating the limousine driver – Paramjit Multani – and the telephone numbers related to Donald Young and Senator Obama. I leave you with these questions that I have asked of Senator Obama of which he has refused to an-

171

swer:

1. Why won't Senator Obama provide his cell phone numbers and telephone records for his personal and official cell phones held by him for the time period of November 3, 1999 through November 8, 1999, when we met?

2. Why won't Senator Obama provide his cell phone numbers and telephone records for his personal and official cell phones held by Senator Obama for September 2007through December 23, 2008, the murder of Donald Young?

3. Why won't Senator Obama provide all email communications both personal and campaign related to and/or from AKP Message & Media from January 18, 2008 through February 29, 2008 for Senator Obama, David Axelrod and David Plouffe?

4. Why won't Senator Obama provide proof of all payments made from AKP Message & Media, Obama for America, David Axelrod, David Plouffe, and Senator Obama's accounts for the period of January 18, 2008 through February 29, 2008?

On my website – larrysinclair.org – you will find the documents that I have referred to in this statement. A copy of the home page for that website is attached.

Thank you for your time and attention this afternoon and I will now take any questions.

After making the above statement, I spent a little more than an hour answering questions from the press in the room. Contrary to the claims on the internet by the pro-Obama groups and publications, the Holeman Lounge was filled for this press conference. After the press conference, I returned to the enclosed bar area between the Holeman Lounge and the First Amendment Room as instructed by the National Press Club. While packing up my laptop and other material used during the press conference, NPC Assistant GM David King and NPC Security Director entered the bar with three men and introduced them as detectives from the D.C. Metro Police.

These men proceeded to inform me that they were there to arrest me on an outstanding warrant from Delaware. My Attorney Montgomery Blair Sibley, who was in the room at the time, asked the men "who are you?" The D.C. police detectives then asked Sibley who he was at which he responded, "I am Mr. Sinclair's Attorney." After this exchange both myself and Sibley asked the detectives if they had the arrest warrant. They responded, "its downstairs in the car, we will show it to you when we get downstairs." Just as the detectives were making that statement two uniformed D.C. Metro Police officers stormed into the room (a white male and black female). The female officer was yelling "Lawrence Sinclair" while holding her hand on her gun and the holster strap undone. I simply responded "yes," with the female responding "you are under arrest," at which time the D.C. detectives stepped in telling these uniformed officers they needed to leave. The female officer demanded to know who the detectives were, and it was clear that she was not happy that she would not be photographed taking me out in hand cuffs. While the Obama supporting media outlets Politico, Huffington Post, etc. published immediate articles claiming I had been taken out of the National Press Club in handcuffs, none of that was true.

After making arrangements with my attorney to take my laptop and other items with him, I walked out of the National Press Club carrying my briefcase the same way I had entered. I was not in hand-cuffs as was reported by the so called reputable media outlets like Politico etc. The D.C. detectives made it clear they (unlike the black female uniformed officer who went storming into the NPC) had no desire to create any type of scene by taking me out in cuffs, or by leaving any other way than by the same keyed elevator in the back of the NPC that I had entered from. Upon arriving in the parking garage shared by the National Press Building and the J.W. Marriott Hotel, the detectives asked me to leave all of my identification, belt, tie, and other personal items with my attorney. At the same time, I had again asked the detectives to show us the arrest warrant. Still no warrant was produced, and again we were told it was somewhere in the car. In the J.W. Marriott garage, I turned over all of my personal belongings and identification to my attorney and went with two of the three detectives in an unmarked black SUV to D.C. Police District One.

After arriving at District One an African American detective who was doing the paperwork on my arrest loaned me his cell phone to call my mother, my hotel and a Pennsylvania lawyer who was to find me an attorney in Delaware. When speaking with the Pennsylvania contact I was asked for the warrant number. I then asked the detective for the warrant number only to be told he did not have it. Shortly after this I was taken to a holding area for the booking process. While awaiting booking the District One jail had been notified of my medical conditions and medications being taken. When I had asked about being given access to my medications I was told several things. First, I was told that I would have to be taken to a hospital if I needed my medications. Then I was told if I went to the hospital, I would run the risk of not making my appearance in court the next day, and I would be stuck in Central Holding until I went before the Judge. I agreed to try and make it until after the booking process was completed. As I was taken into the booking room, I was digitally finger-printed by the D.C. Police. Once my prints were scanned the booking officer printed off a sheet asking me to sign it. While looking at the sheet I noticed that it contained my birth date as being July 23, 1963. When I pointed out that the information about me was incorrect I was told, "That is what the FBI has in their system based on your finger prints and that is what the D.C. Police goes by." After booking was completed, I was taken to Georgetown University Hospital and after about 3 hours of being chained to a metal bench waiting to be seen, the physician refused to do anything other than give me a Tylenol tablet.

On June 19, 2008 I was taken before the D.C.Superior Court Magistrate Judge, Aida L. Melendez, where Judge Melendez, the U.S. Attorney for the District of Columbia, or any-one else asked the single question required by law: "Mr. Sinclair, is the person named on the Delaware warrant you?" The reason Judge Melendez never asked that question is because there was **no** such "Fugitive Warrant" from Delaware. The fact is the D.C. Police with instruction of the D.C. U.S. Attorney, arrested me under false pretense, and then charged me with being a "fugitive from justice," using a manufactured Beau Biden Delaware case as its justification.

SUPERIOR COURT OF THE DISTRICT OF COLUMBIA   L-23

STATE OF DELAWARE   PDID NO. 612643

vs   SP NO.   3834

SINCLAIR, LAWRENCE WAYNE

ORDER FOR RETURN OF FUGITIVE UPON WAIVER

SINCLAIR, LAWRENCE WAYNE   , having appeared with Counsel in open Court

on   JUNE 19, 2008   and having waived further proceedings pursuant

to law and indicated his desire to return voluntarily to the State of DELAWARE   ,
is hereby

ORDERED detained at the District of Columbia Jail pending return to the State of

DELAWARE   .in the custody of the proper officials of that state; and it is

FURTHER ORDERED that SINCLAIR, LAWRENCE WAYNE   has not been

surrendered to the custody of a proper official of the State of DELAWARE

by JUNE 24, 2008   (3 days, not including Saturday, Sunday or holidays), he shall

be returned FORTHWITH to this Court for such further proceedings as the Court shall deem

appropriate.

         6/19/08   _____
            DATE   JUDGE

                              RETURN

OFFICIAL: _____
                           NAME

          _____
                         ADDRESS

          _____
                           TITLE

          WHITE-COURT COPY
          YELLOW-DEFENDANT'S COPY
          PINK-JAIL COPY
          GOLDENROD-COPY TO BE RETURNED TO COURT
                    AFTER EXECUTED

Judge Melendez ordered me held in the District of Columbia De-

partment of Corrections for 72 hours (excluding the date of my

arrest and the date I appeared before the Judge) to allow Dela-

ware time to pick me up. Based on this false arrest I was held in a

D.C. jail from June 18, 2008 to June 23, 2008. I was denied ac-

cess to my medications, denied access to any phone, and denied

177

access to my attorney either in person or by phone. All of this without anyone, including Judge Melendez, ever having produced a copy of any "fugitive from justice" warrant from Delaware.

On June 23, 2008 I was picked up by a representative of the Delaware Attorney General's office and driven to Wilmington. On the drive to Wilmington this Attorney General representative informed me that there was no "fugitive from justice" warrant from Delaware. He said that normally the D.C. Court would have released me with instructions to report to Delaware." After arriving in Wilmington, I went before a Judge in the New Castle County Superior Court and was immediately released on an unsecured bond of $3000.00 (meaning I was immediately released on my word that I would return for any and all court dates). This could have been done six days earlier had D.C. Superior Court Magistrate Judge Aida L. Melendez granted the request made on June 19, 2008 to be released and allowed to take Amtrak from D.C. to Wilmington, Delaware that day. Instead she allowed the U.S. Attorney to request a $700,000 bail.

On June 23, 2008 the New Castle County Superior Court Judge had been informed that Wilmington, Delaware Attorney Richard "Dick" Weir had contacted the court and stated he would be representing me but simply was unable to get to this first appearance. After leaving the courthouse, I was basically stuck in

Wilmington. I had none of my ID or credit cards or anything on me. Money had to be sent to me via Western Union in order for me to get back to D.C. and pick up my ID, laptop and belongings. I remained in D.C. for a couple of days before returning to Delaware traveling on the exact same Amtrak train and car as Joe Biden. In the meantime, the likes of Huffington Post, Politico and others pandering to Barack Obama were publishing outlandish and false statements claiming I was arrested for insurance fraud among other things.

After returning to Washington, D.C. to recover my personal belongings, I received notice that the Social Security Administration had sent a letter dated June 16, 2008 informing me that my disability payments were being terminated because they had been provided information that I was a fugitive from justice from a probation and/or a parole violation." The letter from Social Security originated from its Chicago area office and was dated two days before the June 18, 2008 press conference. When I contacted Social Security, I was told they were contacted on June 16, 2008 and given information that turned out to be *FALSE*. Since when does Social Security or any other federal agency take any type of action on the same day they are contacted, unless the person making that contact is a U.S. Senator named Joe Biden and or Barack Obama?

On June 25, 2008 I left Washington, D.C. to return to Delaware to await my July 3, 2008 court date. I had already missed my return flight from D.C. to Minnesota. The cost of returning to my home in Duluth and back to Wilmington, Delaware for a 5 minute court appearance on July 3, 2008 was far more costly. I spent ten days in Claymont, Delaware interviewing with attorneys, and I finally thought that I had an agreement. Former Delaware Attorney General Richard R. Wier, Jr. had agreed to represent me and on July 2, 2003, we signed said agreement. Then all hell broke loose. At approximately 5:00 PM on July 2, 2008 I received a phone call from Richard Wier screaming at me telling me that he was not going to represent anyone who said the kind of things that I have said about Barack Obama and Joe Biden. We were scheduled to appear in court the very next morning at 8:30 AM! Then Wier started telling me that his office phone has been ringing off the hook with people threatening him. Wier stated, "I am not willing to put my practice and reputation on the line to represent you." And with that Mr. Wier instructed me to appear before the Judge on July 3, 2008 and lie. He said, "Go to court in the morning and tell the Judge that you need more time. Tell the Judge that you have been unable to retain counsel." At this time I told Mr. Wier, "I will appear in the morning, but I will do so make it clear to the Judge that you contacted me after 5:00 PM the day before court telling me you will not show after having signed an agreement to do so."

On July 3, 2008 I appeared in the New Castle County Superior Court for all of five minutes at which time I was given a continuance to July 18, 2008. After leaving court, I met with Newark, Delaware Attorney Francis E. Farren, and retained him to defend me against the Delaware charge of "theft." It should be noted that the court file or the Delaware Attorney General's office provided me or my Attorney Francis Farren with any information as to what I was being accused of stealing until late July 2008. However, the Delaware News Journal Newspaper in Wilmington wasted no time in publishing two articles claiming court records said "Sinclair paid for a three week stay at the RodeWay Inn with counterfeit money orders." Even though the Delaware News Journal was provided credit card statements showing I had paid for my stay with my VISA card. Not to mention the fact that David Ledford, Executive Editor, Delaware News Journal was asked to show a just one court document that made the claims his paper was reporting. Mr. Ledford refused and claimed the News Journal got its information from the Delaware State Troopers media information officer. For almost a year, calls to the Delaware State Troopers media information office have not been returned despite repeated requests for their comment.

From July 2008 through August 27, 2008 I was threatened

by Deputy Delaware Attorney General Susan S. Dwyer with "Life in Prison" if I did not agree to plead guilty to misdemeanor theft on the Delaware indictment. Each time that threat was made, I instructed my Newark, Delaware attorney Francis E. Farren, to inform Ms. Dwyer that I will see here at trial. I was required to travel to Wilmington, Delaware for a "Case Review" scheduled for August 11, 2008. It was made clear this court date was for nothing more than Susan D. Dwyer to offer me the same deal that she did before. I made it clear to Mr. Farren, that "*I will not plead guilty to any charge of any kind.*" After turning down the Attorney General's offer before the Judge, I returned home to Duluth, Minnesota to await the Delaware Attorney General's compliance with the Discovery Request (which she still had not turned over). At the August 11, 2008 Case Review Hearing Attorney Farren provided me a copy of the "Scheduling Order" which had set my trial date for September 11, 2008! Before we went to trial, there would be a final case review which was scheduled for September 2, 2008.

My choice of Francis Farren as legal counsel proved to be an excellent one. It was in late August 2008 when Deputy Attorney General Susan Dwyer provided Mr. Farren with police reports from October 2007. Upon review of the reports, I pointed out to Mr. Farren exactly what I had told him before we were given the reports. I was paid money that was owed to me by Money Orders sent to my Laredo Texas address by UPS. I did not use them to pay for anything. I had a written agreement to deposit them into the account of an individual with an expressly written agreement, that "I will not receive any funds from these items until said items clear the bank." There was also another part of that agreement which the Delaware Attorney General failed to reveal to its "Grand Jury" which stated, "I agree to pay any and all fees if the Money Orders are returned unpaid for any reason." To top all of this, the Delaware Attorney General Beau Biden and Susan S. Dwyer knew before ever bringing a Grand Jury together, that the claim by the depositor of the money orders was absolutely false. This depositor claimed that he had not seen me or spoken with me after he paid me the money from the money orders. This was a blatant lie. In fact, I was at his business on a daily basis and in daily phone contact with him and his employee, who I was driving to and from work. This alone demonstrates that the Delaware Attorney General knew that **NO** crime had ever been committed by me. But they still sought an indictment in February 2008, after I posted my claims about Barack Obama. The Delaware Attorney General Beau Biden and Susan S. Dwyer were acting on information provided to them by a privately hired investigator.

Attorney Francis E. Farren had his job cut out for him. The Obama surrogates and supporters were having spasms because I had not been scared into making a plea deal. These same people who provided false information to the Delaware News Journal, and claiming to be in personal communication with Deputy AG Susan Dwyer, started emailing threats to Ms. Dwyer using my name and email information. In fact, Ms. Dwyer and her supervisor accused me of sending her threatening emails, which I responded to immediately on the blog. Just a day or so after accusing me of sending her threats Ms. Dwyer sent an email to Mr. Farren asking him, "Is Mr. Sinclair willing to risk a life sentence for being a habitual offender if I win at trial?" I responded on the blog to Ms. Dwyer's question. *"YES!"* On August 26, 2008 while working with Mr. Farren on travel arrangements for the September 2nd Case Review, I was told to "Stop, do not make any travel arrangements."

Francis Farren had to deal with the Delaware News Journal publishing false reports about what I was supposed to be charged with; he had to deal with a client who refuses to back down from a fight; he had to deal with a Deputy Attorney General trying to make a name for herself. This Deputy AG did intentionally and falsely accuse me of sending threatening emails. She also provided false and misleading information to the media and bloggers. He indeed had his hands full. Most importantly, he had to keep his sanity, which he DID. Mr. Farren read the claims posted on the internet alleging that he had spoken with these people even though he never did. He did receive an email or two from the Obama bloggers which he laughed at. Francis Farren was prepared to defend me before a jury in Wilmington, Delaware on September 11, 2008. Instead, Mr. Farren was contacted by Susan S. Dwyer, Deputy Delaware Attorney General on August 26, 2008 and told the charges would be dropped ten minutes after Mr. Farren called her requesting a copy of a signed ten page document provided to the depositor of the Money Orders. Money Orders defrauded me!

On August 28, 2008 the formal dismissal of charges was filed in the New Castle County Superior Court in Wilmington, Delaware.

IN THE SUPERIOR COURT OF THE STATE OF DELAWARE

IN AND FOR NEW CASTLE COUNTY

THE STATE OF DELAWARE   )

        VS.   )   NOTICE OF NOLLE PROSEQUI

LAWRENCE W SINCLAIR   )

09/26/1961

                        AG Case Number - NC08000671

A Nolle Prosequi is hereby entered on the charge of:

0712005646 001   IN08020080W * THEFT $1000 OR>

against the above named defendant and the Prothonotary is
requested to note the same on record.

REASON: (18) INSUFFICIENT EVIDENCE

DATED   August 27, 2008

                                SUSAN S DWYER
                                Deputy Attorney General

The charges were dismissed three days after my web sites were taken down due to Denial of Service attacks on August 24, 2008. Charges were dismissed on the very day that I received an email from a participant at the Democratic National Convention in Denver informing me, "Beau Biden was taken into a meeting with high level Obama advisors and told to 'get rid' of the charges against you." "Biden was told that the arrest and filing of the charges had served the purpose of discrediting your June press conference, and the campaign does not want the publicity that a September 11, 2008 trial will bring. Make it go away now," the email continued.

The Delaware Attorney General, Beau Biden, son of now VP Joe Biden along with his father did use an Obama campaign worker to bring an indictment against me for a crime that never happened. Then Senator Joe Biden abused the power of his U.S. Senate Office to knowingly and intentionally provide the Social Security Administration with false information generated by his son. Done for the purpose of harassment and denying me my sole means of survival. Joe and Beau Biden along with D.C. U.S. Attorney had me arrested and held in jail for five to six days without access to my attorney, my required medication and medical care, for no other reason than to try and do damage control for Barack Obama. In exchange, the office of Vice President went to Biden

II, and the Delaware U.S. Senate Seat is waiting for Joseph R. (Beau) Biden III. Remember the words of Jill Biden on Oprah, *"**Joe had his choice of any office he wanted.**"*

Francis E. Farren, Esq. defended me against all odds and he never once tried to talk me into making or accepting any deals. I told Mr. Farren at our first meeting on July 3, 2008, "I am not guilty of any crime, and I will not plead guilty to any crime no matter what they threaten me with." "My whole life I have always admitted to what I have done, and I have always fought when I did not do it. I am fighting this." Mr. Farren did not let the threats or harassments made against him, scare him. Sadly, the same cannot be said for Richard R. Wier, Jr.

To this day, Mr. Farren reminds anyone that asks, "Larry Sinclair was threatened with his life, and he still stood his ground".

Chapter Thirteen
The Physical Description

Over the past year, many people have wanted me to give the details of Barack Obama's "manhood." Not only that, they wanted it posted on the internet so they could edit, misrepresent and hide the truth.

I invited Obama to submit to a private independent exam to verify my description.

I mailed the following letter to Michelle Obama via United States Postal Service overnight Express mail on January 16, 2009.

Lawrence W. Sinclair
Post Office Box 4671
Ft. Walton Beach, FL 32549
(202) 657-4868
Minnman0926@aol.com
www.larrysinclair-0926.blogspot.com

January 15, 2009

Michelle Robinson Obama
Blair House
1651 Pennsylvania Ave NW
Washington, DC 20500

RE: Physical Description

Dear Michelle Robinson Obama:

I am sending you this letter to express my disappointment in your involvement and active participation in the fraud that you and Barry Soetoro have committed and continue to commit on the American people.

You are most certainly not an innocent by-stander in this fraud. In fact, it was you who introduced Barry Soetoro to all the associates, Billy Ayers, Tony Rezko, Mayor Daly, et al.... You brought Jeremiah Wright and Barry together.

I remember you making the following statement in your dig on Hillary Clinton over her husband's affairs, "How can you manage the White House when you can't control your own house."

Well, I have enclosed a physical description of your husband's genitals. I ask you to, publicly, state that the enclosed description is not accurate. I also ask you to take questions concerning your personal knowledge of your husband's sexual encounters with the murdered Donald Young, myself and other men over the course of your marriage. After all, you repeated the call of your husband for openness and transparency. Then let us be open and transparent.

Understand that I will include the enclosed physical de-

scription and this letter in the soon to be released book: BARACK
OBAMA & LARRY SINCLAIR: Cocaine, Sex, Lies & Murder?

Contrary to those obots claims; you are not a victim here;
in fact, you and I both know that you have actively engaged in the
attacks and efforts to shut me up. You had full knowledge of the
relationship between Barry and Donald Young and Barry's use of
Donald Young to get information from me as to who I had told of
Barry's 1999 actions.

I hope that something in your heart of stone might soften,
and you might in the words of Spike Lee, "Do the Right Thing!"

Sincerely,
Lawrence (Larry) Sinclair
"One of the other men in your husband's life."

The United States Postal Service attempted to deliver this
letter and physical description of Barack Obama's genitals on
January 18, 2009, again on January 20, 2009. Both times
Obama's officials refused to accept it. According to the United
States Postal Service online tracking, the letter was finally ac-
cepted on January 26, 2009.

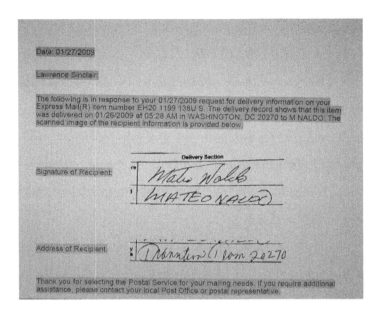

So let us get *down* to some details about Barack Obama's penis. Barack is uncut, or uncircumcised. He was at most approximately eight to eight and a half inches in length. The girth was thin in nature, and had a hook to the left (when facing him). Obama's left testicle clearly hangs lower than his right (the testicle hangs lower but is not larger or smaller in comparison to the right one.) His pubic hairs were shaved.

The most telling part of Barack Obama's penis is that under the head in the split he has (three to be exact) small pimple type bumps. The bumps are not pimples per se, but are under the skin and lead downward on the shaft.

Conclusion

Regardless of what one may think of me; a fact that no one can deny is; I have always admitted my past indiscretions, no matter what the consequences were. Have I lived a perfect life? No. Have I ever blamed my actions in life on others or my surroundings? No. Have I tried to hide my past? No

If you believe the Obama surrogates/supporters, the bloggers and the internet thugs' claims that I am lying, then please explain to me why massive amounts of time, money, and man power have been devoted to relentlessly attacking me for more than a year?

Since January 2008, an against all odds, I have tried to tell my story to hopefully enlighten all Americans to the fact that Barack Obama is nothing more a than a lying, amoral, unethical, two-bit used car salesman. In fact, I am surely insulting car salesmen by comparing them to Obama. He has indeed sold his soul to the Devil in exchange for power, celebrity and wealth. It is still hard for me to believe that half of the American electorate fell under his "charismatic" spell. He is, by far, the best damn TelePrompTer reading President we have ever had!

I stand by my statements about then Senator Barack Hussein Obama purchasing, selling, and using cocaine with me on November 6th and 7th, 1999. I stand by my statements that Barack Obama engaged in Gay sex with me on these same dates. I stand by my statements that I was contacted by the murdered Donald Young and the conversations he had with me.

The bottom line is that no one can say that I am not being truthful, because none of you were there. However, Barack Obama and his organized "machine" know that my states are **TRUE.** Despite the continuing threats, harassment, and personal attacks, I can take complete refuge and serenity in knowing that I am telling the truth; nothing but the truth; so help me God.

"The Truth Will Always Set You Free!"